W9-AZO-829

the bible study
for women only
what you need to know about the inner lives of men

shaunti feldhahn

LifeWay Press® • Nashville, Tennessee

Published by LifeWay Press® • © 2006 Shaunti Feldhahn
Derived from *For Women Only* written by Shaunti Feldhahn, © 2004 Veritas Enterprises, Inc.
Second printing 2008

ISBN 978-1-4158-3217-2
Item 001303673

This book is a resource for course CG-1208 in the Bible Studies Category of the Christian
Growth Study Plan.

Dewey Decimal Classification: 248.843
Subject Headings:WOMEN \ MARRIAGE \ CHRISTIAN LIFE

To order additional copies of this resource, write to LifeWay Church Resources Customer
Service, One LifeWay Plaza, Nashville TN 37234-0113; fax (615) 251-5933; phone toll free
(800) 458-2772; order online at *www.lifeway.com*; e-mail *orderentry@lifeway.com;* or visit the
LifeWay Christian Store serving you.

Printed in the United States of America

Leadership and Adult Publishing
LifeWay Church Resources
One LifeWay Plaza
Nashville, TN 37234-0175

Contents

Shaunti Feldhahn started out as an analyst on Wall Street and ended up a surprise best-selling author. In 2004 her book *For Women Only: What You Need to Know About the Inner Lives of Men* (Multnomah) became a popular conversation-starter for men and women around the country! Several follow-up books are available (*For Men Only*) or in process (*For Young Women Only*, among others).

Shaunti holds a Masters in Public Policy from Harvard University and a Bachelors in Government and Economics from The College of William and Mary in Virginia. In 1998, Shaunti authored a runaway best seller, *Y2K: The Millennium Bug; A Balanced Christian Response*, which was viewed as instrumental in encouraging the Christian community toward a positive, service-oriented response to the approach of the year 2000.

She is also dedicated to writing Christian "message fiction," applying her analysis and research skills to weaving truth-filled and intriguing stories that impact readers on a different level. As a national author and speaker, Shaunti has been featured on Christian and secular media outlets, reaching millions with messages of faith.

On her Web site (*www.shaunti.com*), Shaunti recalls her journey of faith: "When I was 21 years old, about to graduate from college, I sat on a hill overlooking a beautiful lake in Virginia and experienced something that profoundly changed my life. I had grown up in a loving church, with loving parents, and had always believed God existed. I considered myself a good person. But until that day I had never understood why I needed a Savior.

"God was more my consultant than my King, but I figured the good stuff I did outweighed the bad. … I assumed that that meant I'd go to heaven and be with God eventually. I came to Jesus when He made himself so real to me that I knew that all the stories I'd heard my whole life were true. On that sunny Virginia day, I knew He was real, and He was speaking to me. My life changed forever. "

Shaunti lives in Atlanta with her husband, Jeff, and two young children. "I'm amazed at what God has done in my life, how He has blessed me. I have a wonderful husband, two beautiful children, terrific friends. I'm an author, speaker, policy analyst, ministry worker, newspaper columnist, marketing writer… but most of all, I'm a child of the King. I pray that my life will serve Him the way He deserves, and that you, the reader, will know His good news for yourself."

Wanda F. King assisted Shaunti in developing the Bible study framework and concepts, personal learning activities, and leader guide for this resource.

Wanda has been a pastor's wife for more than 30 years. She and her husband, Carl, reared two sons and a daughter on the mission field in Brazil, where they served for 16 years as representatives with the International Mission Board. For 12 years Wanda has written LifeWay curriculum for children.

As a woman's ministry leader in her Knoxville, Tennessee church, Wanda encourages others to find their places of service in God's kingdom. A niche she enjoys is mentoring and teaching through Christian Women's Job Corps. She often has the opportunity to put her Masters of Counseling degree to work helping women or couples overcome personal issues.

I started my amazing journey several years ago, when I stumbled across several fascinating surprises about men. Because I am an analyst by training, I set out to quantify what I was learning and put it all in the little hardcover book that forms the basis for this study, *For Women Only: What You Need to Know About the Inner Lives of Men*. It quickly became a best seller, and I just as quickly got very busy! I started traveling a lot, presenting these findings to church and corporate groups. And though travel can be tiring, it was worth every minute when women would tell me, through tears, how God had opened their eyes to things they desperately needed to see.

But something was missing. I kept hearing from women who were saying, "This information is radically new, and affects everything in my relationship. I need more help to apply it to my life!" Women needed a Bible study about these findings—some way to join together in the study, practice, sharing, and accountability that leads to lasting change. But how to accomplish that? I didn't have the skills to develop something of that magnitude.

But behind the scenes, as He often works, God had a terrific answer! LifeWay Christian Resources approached me about developing a Bible study *together*. I had done many Beth Moore studies and was so humbled to have the opportunity to work with the same wonderful organization that develops those and other women's studies.

Now, after nearly a year of intensive work, I am particularly grateful to Wanda King, who searched the Scriptures to understand and present God's thoughts about the men in our lives and how we can honor each other in our relationships. Wanda's sweet spirit, razor-sharp insight, and excellent writing have been wonderfully used by God in developing so much of this study.

It has also been a privilege to work with everyone on this LifeWay team, especially editor-in-chief Sharon Roberts and executive producer Debbie Beavers, who had such patience with my many idiosyncrasies (that's code for being annoyingly detail-oriented!) during this long process. It has been a joy and an honor to work with you all.

Ladies, I know we're at different places as we start our journey together. Some of you are in great relationships, others in very difficult ones, and still others in no particular romantic relationship right now. Some women may find these revelations fun, fascinating, or con-victing; while others of you may find them very hard to hear and even harder to accept.

I understand those feelings because I have experienced them at one time or another in my research… and even today. Even though I wrote the book, I still have to make that essential choice, every day, to not only discover what God would have me learn about my husband's needs, but also to actually do something about it. Here, then, is my prayer for us all:

Dear, sweet Lord, You are the Author of love and You delight in Your children.
And You want for us the delights that come when we follow Your ways—even when
they stretch us. Give us teachable minds to hear Your voice as we learn and willing hearts
to apply it to the men You have placed in our lives. We love You and thank You that
You know the plans You have for us and that You want to give us a future and a hope.
Thank You for Your precious gift of love. Amen.

Welcome to *For Women Only: The Bible Study*. As Shaunti has promised, you are in for an exciting ride!

This study about relationships grows out of Shaunti's popular *For Women Only: What You Need to Know About the Inner Lives of Men*. If you don't know the full (and fascinating) story of how this book came about, you may want to read more at her Web site, *www.shaunti.com*.

Almost by accident Shaunti came across surprising revelations about the inner lives of men—findings that were validated by a groundbreaking nationwide survey and personal interviews with more than 1,000 men. Many women are finding their marriages being strengthened and relationships being restored. *For Women Only: The Bible Study* unpacks biblical principles related to these important findings.

As you begin this seven-week study, keep several things in mind. Each week the material in your book is divided into five days of individual study. In the group session that follows, you will hear more from Shaunti as well as from our own men's focus group (if your group uses the DVD video in the leader kit). You will enjoy sharing your discoveries and questions with other women in your group.

You will gain more by attending each session and participating fully in your group. Begin now to pray for yourself and your husband, your small-group leader, and the other women who will attend this study with you.

Each day's reading takes approximately 30 minutes. Try not to rush this time. The personal learning activities, marked in **bold** or highlighted by icons, can help you apply what you are learning. Here are some features:

- In addition to a Lightbulb that describes the focus of the week, the introduction to each week's readings presents a Weekly Challenge to practice. Try to do this work even though it may feel awkward. It will become easier with practice!
- When you see the Spotlight icon, it's time to place yourself in his shoes for a while. Putting yourself in his place will go a long way to helping you understand how your husband feels deep inside.
- The Searchlight icon, at the end of daily readings, helps you examine your thoughts, feelings, or actions and to see ways God is working in your life.
- Most daily readings include a "So What Do I Do?" section. As you begin to see areas in which you might need to change how you relate to your man, this is a logical question to ask. So this content offers practical tips to help you put your new knowledge and insights into practice.

For the facilitator of a *For Women Only* group, the leader guide in the back of this book (pp. 161-171) provides a teaching plan for each group session.

You are in for an exciting ride as you give God permission to change *you!* At the same time, be on the lookout for ways *your man* is becoming the man God intended him to be from the very beginning!

Unraveling the Mystery of Manhood

This study is all about going from a _____ understanding to what it means in _____ .

> *"Use wisdom and understanding to establish your home;*
> *let good sense fill the rooms with priceless treasures.*
> *Wisdom brings strength, and knowledge gives power" (Prov. 24:3-5, CEV).*

The Bible tells us the value of _____ , _____ ,
_____ , and _____ _____ .

What do wisdom and understanding do? (_____ _____ _____ well)

What do wisdom and knowledge bring? (_____ and _____)

What does good sense do? (fills the rooms with _____ _____)

Knowledge = learning something new

Understanding = internalizing new information

Wisdom = gaining insight into how to make something work

Good sense = moving from theory to reality

Ground rules

1. We will honor our men—no male bashing.
2. What is said in your group stays in your group.
3. We will talk about what is *common* to men—not necessarily what is right.
4. These are generalizations and there will always be exceptions.
5. This study is not about what he should know and do, but about what we should know and do. It is intentionally *one - sided* .
6. This study is not a substitute for counseling.

❏ Are you willing to be one-sided?

❏ Are you willing to give God permission to:

Change your mind? Change your actions?

Are you willing? If so, check your commitments.

"Be transformed by the renewing of your mind" (Rom. 12:2).

week one

"If you had to choose, would you rather feel alone and unloved in the world OR would you rather feel inadequate and disrespected by everyone?" *What kind of choice is that?*, I remember thinking, probably like most of the other women attending that singles retreat years ago. *Who would ever choose to feel unloved?* Were we ever in for a surprise.

The retreat speaker turned to the men's side of the room. "OK, men. Who here would rather feel alone and unloved?" A sea of hands went up, and a gasp rippled across the women's side of the room. He then asked which men would rather feel disrespected, and we women watched in bemusement as only a few guys lifted their hands. Then it was our turn to answer and the men's turn to be shocked when most of the women indicated they would rather feel inadequate and disrespected than unloved.

It may sound like a no-brainer ... but men and women are different! We cannot begin to count all the books and articles that have been written about the differences between us—differences in our emotions, our love languages, our personalities. Scientists even study how differently our brains function!

We know we are different; yet, we sometimes act as though we are not. We often relate as if our man's needs are the same as our own. Our journey together these next few weeks will challenge some of our assumptions.

Years after that landmark singles retreat, the research behind the trade book *For Women Only* tested this same question, among others. And the answers we received from these men were equally astounding. Seventy-four percent of those surveyed indicated they too would rather feel alone and unloved than disrespected or inadequate. Men and women appear to differ in this fundamental way: Women think in terms of love while men need respect.

In tallying the research results, a major lightbulb came on for me: *If a man feels disrespected, he is going to feel unloved.* And what that translates to is this: If you want to love your man in the way he needs to be loved, then you need to ensure that he feels your respect most of all. This surprising outcome affects many other discoveries we will share.

Appropriately, then, the first element of the inner life of men to enter our study is also your first Lighbulb. It is a foundational concept:

Men would rather feel unloved than inadequate and disrespected.
Men most need respect.

During this study, we'll have the privilege of placing ourselves under the scrutiny and discernment of the Holy Spirit. We'll see what the Bible has to say about Christ-honoring relationships. (While our primary application is to marriage, singles will benefit, too. I use the term "your man" a lot to include both single and married women.)

We'll learn from men in the eye-opening interviews and research that were part of *For Women Only,* and we'll hear from some guys in our video. We'll start at the very beginning as we consider God's plan for men and women.

So here we go. Prayerfully expect lightbulbs to come on in your thoughts and actions. Cast the spotlight on your relationship with your man. Point the searchlight of Scripture to your relationship with God and with your man. We'll give you some reminders along the way.

Lightbulb

Anytime you see this symbol in your workbook, be on the lookout for a revelation about the sometimes-surprising common inner wiring of men. Make your discovery personal by asking, *What do I need to do as a result?*

Spotlight

This is a call to put yourself in your husband's place. Focus your attention on what he is thinking and feeling.

Searchlight

This feature will help you ask God to reveal the changes *you* need to make and then to give you the strength to do it! Using this workbook like a journal can help you see how God is working in your life.

Our feelings often follow our actions, meaning we can begin taking the hard steps we know to take even when our feelings aren't there yet! That is why we have Weekly Challenges: to give you an attitude or action to practice on your own or with your man. Giving priority to these Weekly Challenges will begin to change you … which is what this study is all about, isn't it?

Weekly Challenge

Your first challenge is: Choose to respect your man by not saying anything negative to him or about him to others. Begin each day with prayer that God will help you meet this new challenge.

We hear a lot about love today. Love is good, and women are usually good at loving. However, many men admit that, while they know the women in their lives love them, something is still lacking.

Lightbulb
A man's greatest need is to feel respected.

Our Differences Are Very Good

So God made the wildlife of the earth according to their kinds, the livestock according to their kinds, and creatures that crawl on the ground according to their kinds. And God saw that it was good.
Genesis 1:25

As women, we often think we know many things about our man's inner life. But once we go below the surface and into specifics, everything changes. Let's start at the beginning—and I do mean, The Very Beginning, with the creation account—for some revealing insights.

How did God evaluate His creation? (See Gen. 1:25.)

_____

After He created humans? (See Gen. 1:31.)

_____

God saw all that He had made, and it was very good. Evening came, and then morning: the sixth day.
Genesis 1:31

God created us in His own image, and He created us male and female. Our differences have been there from the beginning, and they are "very good."

Read Genesis 2 in your Bible, looking for some practical differences between men and women. According to Genesis 2:7-8,15, where did God place Adam and what did He expect him to do?

_____

By creating Eve, what need did God meet for Adam? (See Gen. 2:18,20-24.)

_____

God put Adam in the garden to oversee it and care for it. God created Eve as a helpmeet for Adam. He was overjoyed with and awed by her, but then came the Fall and God's judgments on our sin. Suddenly, being a man or a woman became more complicated.

Continue in your Bible to Genesis 3:16-19. Place a *w* beside the consequences God gave to the woman and an *m* beside the consequences of sin for the man.

____ Childbirth is marked by pain   ____ The ground is cursed
____ One desires the other   ____ Work is painful
____ Making a living is   ____ The other will rule over you
      difficult work

To the woman, God declared that even with the pain of childbirth, she would long for her husband with desire and her husband would exert authority in the relationship. The female's focus tends to be on relationship. Do we not constantly seek love and assurance from our man? In general, while our personal priorities may differ, in relationships what we want more than anything is for him to love us!

For the man, God's punishment not only included personal consequences but also a curse on all creation. The very ground would produce obstacles that would make it trying just to live. Just as Adam went from illustrious overseer to shameful laborer, so would man be forever competing to get back on top. The never-ending struggle to claim respect for himself had begun.

His focus is on survival, on what he produces. Our man wants and needs our respect.

Respect Is the Key

According to Merriam-Webster Online Dictionary, to respect someone is "to consider (that person) worthy of high regard" or to "esteem" him. Interestingly, *respect* also encompasses the idea "to refrain from interfering with."[1] Our study together will reveal some ways we unintentionally "interfere with," or disrespect, our man.

While women relate to men in a variety of roles (father, son, co-worker), all would agree that marriage is the crucible for male/female relationships. Notice that one of the classic biblical passages on marriage—Ephesians 5—never tells the wife to love her husband.

Read Ephesians 5:33 in the margin for what it tells her to do instead. Circle the key word.

To sum up, each one of you is to love his wife as himself, and the wife is to respect her husband.
Ephesians 5:33

This conclusion to Ephesians 5 urges the husband to *love* his wife and the wife to *respect* her husband and his leadership. Have you ever noticed this distinction? Just as you yearn to hear your man say, "I love you," so does he long to hear words that let him know you respect and esteem him. For a moment, look at Ephesians 5:33 not as a command but as a divine insight into your man's needs. In this verse, God is giving us a glimpse into the schematic of a man's inner life.

Check the feelings you experience when your husband does something that makes you feel truly loved and desired.

❏ warm fuzzies   ❏ proud   ❏ selfish   ❏ vengeful
❏ kind-hearted   ❏ generous   ❏ happy   ❏ glowing

You know what it does to you when your husband does something that makes you feel loved and desired. Now, let's get in his shoes to internalize how wonderful your respect makes him feel. Job, "the greatest man among all the people of the east" (Job 1:3b), offers us a great character study.

Talk about respect; here is a man about whom God Himself boasted, a man of integrity! (See Job 1:1). God trusted Job so much that he allowed some pretty heavy trials to come into his life. Job lost his oxen, his sheep, his camels, his servants, and even his children. Everyone was asking Job what he had done wrong. In his cry of innocence, Job looked back to better days.

Read Job 29 in your Bible. Look for indicators that people respected Job, and then check two that are important to your man.

❑ People spoke well of him.
❑ People listened to and respected his words.
❑ People acknowledged his justice and compassion toward the needy.
❑ People looked to him for advice.
❑ Other: _____

Job was on top of his game. Can't you just picture his confidence? As long as he was seen as one who could do the job, he could hold his own with the best of them. His generosity knew no bounds, and he was held in high esteem.

Things seemed to come easily to Job. He conquered challenges with ease (see v. 17). He extended kindness and fairness in such a way that people characterized him as wise and just (see v. 12). He directed others, and they responded to his leadership and righteousness (see vv. 14-16,25). He resolved conflicts. He was rejuvenated.

Review the indicators of respect that you checked as important to your man. How do they put him on "top of his game"?

_____

When your man feels respected, every aspect of his life is affected. The inner life of a man is a package, with all the elements wrapped up together. Whether you are relating to a husband, a boyfriend, or a son, it is impossible to understand one part of a man's inner life in isolation. Every area affects every other area. However, you can be sure that respect is the foundation upon which all the others rest.

The rub is that, at times, showing him respect means giving up a little. Sometimes we may have to demonstrate respect even when he is not meeting our expectations.

*Just as you want
others to do for you,
do the same for them.*
Luke 6:31

According to Jesus in Luke 6:31, what is the starting point for showing respect to others?

_____

A godly relationship is about putting someone else's needs above your own in obedience to Christ. Marriage is about putting the other person's needs above your own (he's required to do that, too), and it does tremendous things for your husband to know that you are choosing to trust and honor him.

The funny thing is—most of us do respect the men in our lives and often don't realize when our words or actions convey exactly the opposite! In the coming weeks we'll see much more clearly when and how this happens. We women often tend to want to control things, which, unfortunately, guys tend to interpret as disrespect and distrust. (If we're honest with ourselves, it sometimes is.) When we understand respect, we will also be better able to recognize when we are moving too far along on the disrespect barometer.

Where Are You on the Disrespect Barometer?

In coming weeks you will receive a great deal of insight as you hear from men themselves about how they are feeling and what they are thinking. I am going to suggest examples of what to say or do and what not to say or do. And you will want to practice a lot! But first let's use your responses to two questions to clue you in on a surefire "disrespect barometer."

If you are in an emotional conflict with the man in your life, is it acceptable for you to break down and cry? ❏ yes ❏ no

In the same conflict, is it OK for him to get angry? ❏ yes ❏ no

Most of us probably answered, "Yes, it's OK for me to cry." But while crying makes sense to us, we often have a problem with his getting angry. We think he's out of control or behaving improperly.

Dr. Emerson Eggerichs, founder of Love and Respect Ministries, offers a different interpretation. "In a relationship conflict, crying is often a woman's response to feeling unloved, and anger is often a man's response to feeling disrespected."[2] So one way to know when you've crossed the disrespect line is to check for anger.

Just like you, a man may not be able to articulate his feelings in the heat of the moment. He won't necessarily blurt out something helpful like, "You're disrespecting me!" But rest assured, if he's angry at something you have said or done and you don't understand why, there is a good chance he is feeling the pain or humiliation of your disrespect. More than 80 percent of men in the *For Women Only* research said that in a conflict they are likely to be feeling disrespected. Whereas we girls are far more likely to be wailing, "He doesn't love me!"

Spotlight
Describe a recent time your husband reacted in anger toward you.

_____

_____

Could he have been feeling disrespected?
❏ yes ❏ no ❏ It's a possibility
Jot down any additional insights God brings to your mind.

_____

_____

_____

Keeping a record of what God reveals to you during this study will be a great tool for marking your personal and spiritual growth.

He Cannot Demand Your Respect

When your man feels disrespected, you may not hear him telling you so. However, you may see him begin to wilt (figuratively) before your eyes. Or that little muscle in his jaw starts to work. He may not only have trouble articulating his feelings, he also may not feel, in good conscience, that he can demand your respect.

And he's on target; respect cannot be demanded, it can only be given. So he probably won't feel your respect unless you choose to give it to him.

It is not good to eat too much honey, or to seek glory after glory.
Proverbs 25:27

Proverbs 25:27 says too much honey isn't good for anyone. What else is not good for us?

_____

OK, maybe you can eat a lot of honey; however, the second part of this verse tells us it is not good to "seek glory after glory."

After reading Luke 14:7-11, write what Jesus taught to be the better way.
He told a parable to those who were invited, when He noticed how they would
    choose the best places for themselves:
"When you are invited by someone to a wedding banquet, don't recline at the best place,
    because a more distinguished person than you may have been invited by your host.
The one who invited both of you may come and say to you, 'Give your place to this man,'
    and then in humiliation, you will proceed to take the lowest place.
"But when you are invited, go and recline in the lowest place, so that when the one who
    invited you comes, he will say to you, 'Friend, move up higher.' You will then be honored
    in the presence of all the other guests.
"For everyone who exalts himself will be humbled, and the one who humbles himself
    will be exalted" (Luke 14:7-11).

He also said to the one who had invited Him, "When you give a lunch or a dinner, don't invite your friends, your brothers, your relatives, or your rich neighbors, because they might invite you back, and you would be repaid.

_____

Jesus also taught we are not to seek our own glory; instead, we are to humble ourselves.

On the contrary, when you host a banquet, invite those who are poor, maimed, lame, or blind. And you will be blessed, because they cannot repay you; for you will be repaid at the resurrection of the righteous."
Luke 14:12-14

Check the statement that best reflects the message of Luke 14:12-14 (margin).
❏ Be hospitable and show honor to those individuals whom you know are worthy of recognition.
❏ Be hospitable and show honor to those who have need even though they may not be able to repay you.

Jesus promised that we will be blessed when, like the banquet host, we honor someone who may not deserve it or who cannot reciprocate in kind.

I realize that for some women in this study, your hearts are broken. Some of you are no longer able to respect or value the man in your lives. I urge you to find the additional—and, in some cases, professional—help that you need beyond this study.

At the same time, keeping in mind three points can provide valuable perspective. You may be caught in what Dr. Eggerichs dubs the "crazy cycle"—that unfortunate dynamic in which your man doesn't give enough love, so you don't give enough respect, so he feels slighted and doesn't give enough love … and on and on it goes.

Also, as we mentioned at the beginning of our study, recognize that feelings often follow words or actions, not the other way around. For example, if you regularly disparage your husband to him or to friends, it should not be surprising when you begin to feel contempt for him. When we honor him in our actions, our feelings toward him change too. This is the principle behind our Weekly Challenges.

Finally, we can choose to honor and demonstrate respect to our husbands even if we are in a relationship that makes that choice difficult. I have seen many lives and relationships changed by such a one-sided choice! When we take hard steps, one at a time, they become easier and end up changing our attitudes and our very lives. Watch how God will work in you when you take the first step!

Does this help you make sense out of our week's title, "Your Love Is Not Enough"? Of course, your love is, and will always be, important; but, the man in your life may need your respect as much as, if not more than, your love.

Read again the second verse of this week's memory passage (Rom. 12:1-2), letting it become your course verse and goal:
> *"Do not be conformed to this age,*
> *but be transformed by the renewing of your mind,*
> *so that you may discern what is the*
> *good, pleasing, and perfect will of God."*

Complete the following sentence with the correct word:
Your goal during the next six weeks is to r _____ your mind in Christ and ultimately change your pattern of behavior.

Searchlight

Read Psalm 139:23-24 in your Bible as you close today's study. Pray and ask God to turn a searchlight on your life. Invite God to bring your motives, concerns, and worries to the light. Ask God to help you recognize anything you might be doing that would stand in the way of your man knowing how much you love and respect him.

Surrender your feelings, thoughts, and actions to a godly examination in the next few weeks. Each time you see the Searchlight symbol, get ready to place another part of your heart and life under God's scrutiny. Journaling your thoughts can reveal markers of how God is working in your life.

The most important aspect of demonstrating respect is that it is a choice. Just as our men can choose to demonstrate love toward us even if they don't feel it at the moment, so can we choose to show him respect.

Lightbulb
Showing respect is a choice we make in obedience to God.

Choosing to Obey God

You have learned that God's plan is that the wife respect her husband.

> **Based on your discovery from Ephesians 5:33, fill in the blanks with the appropriate words:**
> "To sum up, each one of you is to love his _____ as himself, and the _____ is to _____ her husband."

Perhaps this verse raised some questions in your mind. Maybe it tugged a bit at your heart. Or did it sit uneasily in the pit of your stomach? God's instructions often convict us to change in some way.

Let me squarely confront an assumption we sometimes make in relationships, but especially in marriage: that love must be unconditional, but respect must be earned. Our husbands are deserving of respect because God *says* they are to be respected. Do we always agree with them? Well, maybe not. But the Bible tells us a wife should show her husband respect. As always with God's Word, the choice is yours. You can obey or not, but today I want to help you see why respect is the godly and right choice.

Think of it this way: on those days when I am definitely unlovable, do I want Jeff to turn his back on me and say, "Shaunti, I can't love you today because you just aren't very lovable"? No, the biblical direction to my husband is that he love me even on my bad days.

But God proves His own love for us in that while we were still sinners Christ died for us!
Romans 5:8

Someone loved you when you didn't deserve it. According to the verse in the margin, who loves you with an unending love, and how was that love demonstrated?

_____

_____

God loved us when we were unworthy and unlovely, not because we deserve His love. I can't earn God's love. Instead, I have to humbly move into the position of being able to receive His grace. I do not deserve God's mercy and forgiveness, but what He did for me through Jesus puts me in the position to be forgiven. I have a life-changing decision to make about Jesus.

Similarly, as my husband, my man has moved into the position of deserving my respect. He does not have to earn it. I am to offer my respect to him willingly and unconditionally.

According to God's Word, the woman is worthy to be loved because she is the wife and the man is worthy of respect because he is the husband. She may not always be lovable and he may not always be worthy of respect but each position deserves a God-ordained response. When you choose to respond to him with respect, you are making the choice to do what God expects.

If you love Me, you will keep My commandments.
John 14:15

Circle in John 14:15 words that explain what God expects of you if you love Him.

Our love for God shows itself in obedience to His commands, including those related to respect and godly relationships.

Choosing the Mind of Christ

I am indeed aware that for some women the choice is harder than for others, but hang in there with me. I want to show you what happens when we make this choice regardless of the fact that it is hard. Does it matter? Yes, very much, because the attitude I am describing is summed up in Philippians 2:5 (NIV): *"Your attitude should be the same as that of Christ Jesus."* Impossible, you say? Read on.

Do nothing out of selfish ambition or vain conceit, but in humility consider others better than yourselves.
Philippians 2:3, NIV

Check the statement that best reflects the practical application of each verse.

Philippians 2:3
❏ I can think of ways to help my husband come out on the winning side.
❏ I deserve recognition when I am right or he's wrong; I am a very capable person.

Philippians 2:4
❏ If I don't stand up for myself and what is important to me, I will get walked over.
❏ My greatest concern should be the best interests of my husband.

Each of you should look not only to your own interests, but also to the interests of others.
Philippians 2:4, NIV

Philippians 2:5-7
❏ My feelings are just as important as his, and I don't want to always give up.
❏ I should follow the example of Jesus, who did not try to hold on to everything He had a right to but humbly took a back seat for a while.

Jesus did not count it loss to give up heaven and to come live as a man on earth to save us. He knew firsthand the significance of these words: *"For whoever wants to save his life will lose it, but whoever loses his life because of Me will find it"* (Matt. 16:25). The good news for us is that this verse is not only about eternal life, but also about abundant living day-to-day!

Your attitude should be the same as that of Christ Jesus, who, being in very nature God, did not consider equality with God something to be grasped, but made himself nothing, taking the very nature of a servant, being made in human likeness.
Philippians 2:5-7, NIV

Day-to-day means making the choice to respect your husband when it goes against your grain. Day-to-day means giving up your right to say "I told you so" when the business deal goes bad. The choice is yours again and again to take on the attitude of Christ and say, "This is what is best for *him* right now."

In essence God is telling us, "Respect is important to your man. Showing him respect will make you happy as his wife. It will make your family work. That's the plan . . . My plan."

Yes, a choice is required of you, but God is so good. He promises us a reward when we obey. That reward may be seeing a wonderful side of your husband you have never seen before as he is being built up into the man God intends. Begin watching for how God is at work in both of you.

Are you beginning to see the difference between respect and disrespect?
❏ yes ❏ no ❏ It's still hard.

Can you recall a time you were disrespectful or conveyed a lack of trust to the man in your life?
❏ yes ❏ no

If yes, jot a word or phrase that reminds you of this situation.

_____

_____

Thank God for this insight … and ask His help to stop doing the disrespectful thing(s) you did! Our trouble comes more often, however, when we respond to men in ways we do not *recognize* as being disrespectful. Remember the disrespect barometer? His anger is your first clue.

Spotlight
Recall something you say to your man that sometimes gets a reaction you don't quite understand. This week ask him what goes through his mind when you make this statement, and jot it down here.

_____

_____

Did you learn something useful?

Making a Life-Changing Choice

In Ephesians 5:33 the Greek word translated as respect, *phobeo*, adds much to our understanding. *Phobeo* means to appreciate, esteem, honor, adore, and value. We're not talking bland regard here, but high esteem.

Rewrite the sentence "I respect my husband (or boyfriend)" three times. Each time replace the word *respect* with one of the translations given.
For example: I <u>appreciate</u> my husband (boyfriend).

1. _____

2. _____

3._____

Do you <u>appreciate</u> the fact that this man has committed himself to a relationship with you?

❏ Most of the time ❏ Occasionally ❏ Never *not often enough*

Can you <u>esteem</u> him as a man who had the good sense to choose you?

❏ Most of the time ❏ Occasionally ❏ Never *yes*

Can you <u>honor</u> him as someone to whom God has given awesome responsibility?

❏ Most of the time ❏ Occasionally ❏ Never *yes*

Do you <u>adore</u> him for who he is as a person?

❏ Most of the time ❏ Occasionally ❏ Never *yes*

Will you <u>value</u> him as a human being just as God values you?

❏ Most of the time ❏ Occasionally ❏ Never

Write in the margin or in the space at the end of this page at least one thing you appreciate, esteem, or value about your man. Find an opportunity before the next group meeting to let him know.

Searchlight

"If then there is any encouragement in Christ, if any consolation of love, if any fellowship with the Spirit, if any affection and mercy, fulfill my joy by thinking the same way, having the same love, sharing the same feelings, focusing on one goal" (Phil. 2:1-2). These verses remind us that the woman who is in Christ has at her disposal, through Him, all that she needs to focus on her goal of respecting her man.

Can you point to a specific time in your life when you accepted Jesus Christ as your personal Lord and Savior? If so, praise Him for the forgiveness, comfort, fellowship, and tenderness that are yours because you are His. Pray that He will help you have the attitude of Christ in relationship to your husband.

If you cannot describe such a personal experience with Jesus, read the verses on page 173. Admit that you are a sinner; repent and believe that God raised Jesus from the dead; and ask Him to be your Savior and Lord. If you have questions about this life-changing decision, please talk to your leader.

Feeling respect for our husbands but not overtly showing it is the same as their feeling love for us but not letting us know! One of the secrets to understanding the inner lives of men is discovering just what is affirming to them. Our words and actions can often leave them feeling distrusted, stupid, or lazy—even when that was not our intention!

May I remind you again: Our focus is on him. Just as there are areas in which you want your man to be ultrasensitive to your needs, you must be willing to recognize that he has issues we may think are silly but that matter a lot to him.

Lightbulb
Men need us to respect their judgment and abilities.

Respect His Judgment

You've heard the old joke: "Why do I have to tell my wife I love her? I told her that when we got married!" Are you, in turn, ever guilty of thinking *I married him, didn't I and I'm still here, aren't I? Of course he knows I respect him.* The truth is, we women often do tend to want to control things which, unfortunately, men can interpret as disrespect or distrust. Remember some of our dictionary definitions of respect? There are times when showing respect means to simply refrain from interfering.

At times, we are only asking for information and he hears us differently. At other times, we are convinced we are right. I can argue my husband into the ground if I think I am right! Oddly enough, most women don't mind when our man argues with us, but because of how he is wired, he minds very much when we argue with him. Hear me on this: No matter what we think we are saying, what matters in the end is what the guy is *hearing*.

In the research, many men said the one thing they wished they could tell their wives was to "show more trust in my decision-making abilities"—which is code for (among other things) "I'm not stupid." While they were not looking for wives with no opinions, many men wished their mates wouldn't question their knowledge or argue with their decisions all the time. A man deeply needs the woman in his life to respect his knowledge, opinions, and decisions—what I call his judgment.

Check all that apply: When he expresses an opinion, do you frequently
- ❏ argue?
- ❏ question his decision?
- ❏ respond with "Oh, but what about …?", "No, that's not right …", or "But why …"?

I want you to know I still do these things too! I need encouragement to do the hard things just as much as you do. So don't give up; we're in this together.

Check all that apply. According to Proverbs 21:9, a nagging wife
- ❏ provides a man much-needed help
- ❏ is to be avoided at all costs
- ❏ describes me occasionally
- ❏ can be found on a nearby rooftop

Better to live on the corner of a roof than to share a house with a nagging wife.
Proverbs 21:9

While the nagging wife is an extreme, the men who were surveyed were real touchy about the issue of his judgment. Several confessed that they felt as if their opinions and decisions were actively valued in every area of their lives except at home. Some men felt that their work colleagues trusted their judgment more than their wives did, and I will bet that their wives were clueless.

Respect His Abilities

Another strong theme that emerged from the research was that men want—even need—to figure things out for themselves. It's fun as well as affirming when they solve the big puzzle. Problem is, we want to help them—and guess how they sometimes interpret that? You've got it: distrust. And sometimes they are correct.

Look at some communication that might be going on at your house. Now I know what you meant, but notice what could be going through your man's brain.

Man and his challenge	Her response	His thought
1. Lost, trying to find his way	1. "Honey, please stop and ask for help."	1. "C'mon—it's fun to find my way. I have a clock on the dash. I know whether we'll be late."
2. Dealing with a plumbing problem	2. "Call the plumber!"	2. "As protector of the home, I want to try this first."
3. Fixing the DVD player	3. "Let me try."	3. "Does she think I'm stupid? Now I *have* to fix it."

You might be asking, "Why can't I tell him how to do it if I know the best way? We're equals, and it gets the job done." Well, of course you can. Remember though, he may hear what you say as a lack of trust, almost as if you view him as an idiot. Frequent media portrayals of men as comical, clumsy clods sometimes reinforce his thinking—and our actions.

Hear the heart cry of one man from the survey who wished he could tell his wife, "Trust my judgment on everyday items. Have confidence in my general abilities of learning, application, fixing, rebuilding, repair without having to do it your way because you know it and think I do not." Are you beginning to see how important it is for you to make the choice to trust and respect him?

 ## Spotlight

Think for a moment about some areas in which your husband would rather have your trust than your advice. Make any notes in the margin to help you remember these thoughts.

When we force ourselves to trust our men in the small things, our efforts are interpreted as signs of our overall trust and respect for them as men. The next time your husband seems to stubbornly drive in circles, ask yourself what is more important: being on time to the party or his feeling trusted. No contest.

So What Do I Do?

Agape (agapao) love means "to love dearly." It is an imperative.

Ladies, changing the way we respond to our husbands so we can meet their deep inner needs is not easy; but, in Christ, you have the resources to do it! Remember what we are so good at—loving! We love because God first loved us. Through His Spirit, we can find the power to respect our man in the way he needs.

Love is patient; love is kind. Love does not envy; is not boastful; is not conceited; does not act improperly; is not selfish; is not provoked; does not keep a record of wrongs; finds no joy in unrighteousness, but rejoices in the truth; bears all things, believes all things, hopes all things, endures all things.
1 Corinthians 13:4-7

Agape love is available to us and through us as Christians. We often read the verses in the margin, 1 Corinthians 13:4-7, wishing, *That's the kind of love I want to receive!* We also can erroneously view these verses as telling us how to love our husbands romantically. Remember, we are to love our man in the way he needs to be loved—by respecting him.

Focusing on him and how he needs to be loved, reread these verses. Match characteristics of *agape* love with efforts you can make to show trust in your man's judgment and abilities.

***Agape* Love Traits**	**Trusting Actions**
a. Unselfish, does not envy	___ Support him in what he is attempting.
b. Not boastful or proud	___ Give up being right all the time.
c. Trusting and kind	___ Let him try.
d. Patient, not easily angered	___ Show confidence in his decisions.
e. Not rude, keeps no record of wrongs	___ Defer to his judgment sometimes.

These areas stretch us, don't they? Are you uncomfortable putting your needs so far in the background? Afraid you will become a doormat or will lose your identity? Do you feel that supporting your man will condone his mistakes?

There is no fear in love; instead, perfect love drives out fear, because fear involves punishment. So the one who fears has not reached perfection in love.
1 John 4:18

According to 1 John 4:18, what is the antidote to fear?

_____

God's perfect love drives away fear. We can extend that kind of love to others because it comes from Him (see 1 John 4:7). I am asking you to be an instrument that delivers to your man the love and respect God says he requires. When you are unsure whether you can trust, defer to, or respect your man, trust God to achieve the victory through you.

> When her husband became a private pilot, Tracie worried about his lack of concern for realistically judging time. She fretted about his unwavering attitude that everything would always work out in his favor. The couple often found themselves in awkward situations that could have been avoided had he listened to her.
>
> Before John left on his first flight, Tracie pleaded," Please promise me that if there is ever any doubt, you won't take off. Promise me you will wait and won't misjudge the amount of time you need." He promised.
>
> A few days later she got a call. John had taken off too late in the day. With no authority to fly at night, he had had to make an emergency landing. He was fine, but the plane was wrecked. Tracie knew by the tone of his voice that her husband was devastated. She had never heard him so despondent.

What do you think John was expecting Tracie to say or do? What would you do?

_____

Now let me tell you the end of this story. Tracie knew that her tendency was to say, "I told you so." After all, she was right again, wasn't she? As she rounded each curve of the long, dusty road to the small town where he was staying, she prayed, "Lord, help me to watch my tongue. Help me to be positive and reassuring. Enable me to help my husband and not say, 'I told you so.'"

Tracie will tell you she doesn't remember what she said when she arrived. However, she does remember a sense of _Wow! I don't sound like I usually do, and I like it. God and I are doing this together._ The Lord had smoothed her rough edges and allowed her words to be a soothing touch instead of an abrasive cut.

You Can Do This!

I hope you are beginning to see that when you decide to trust him this time even though he blew it last time, it is not demeaning to you. You are actually living the love that is taught in 1 Corinthians. Oh, you can try to hold onto your pride and maintain your rights. But according to the Apostle Paul, you gain absolutely nothing if you don't have this kind of love (see 1 Cor. 13:3). Instead of your respect bringing you down, it lifts both of you up.

Will you have to make sacrifices? Probably.

What did God give up for you, according to 1 John 4:10? _____ _____

What are some attitudes or actions you may need to give up in order to show respect for your man's judgment and abilities?

Attitudes	Actions
_____	_____
_____	_____
_____	_____

 ## Searchlight
You can do all things because you have God's love on which to rely and lean. Conclude your study today by reading I John 4:12 in your Bible. Pray, asking God to fill you with His love so that you can make trust choices that are respectful to your man.

Thank God that His perfect love can calm your fears about what you may have to give up. In the margin write characteristics from 1 Corinthians 13 that you most need to cultivate, and ask for His strength in these areas.

In 99.9 percent of relationships, the principles we discuss are hard to do but worth the effort. We want to acknowledge that cases of serious emotional or physical abuse call for more intensive intervention than we can get into here. If you are in such a situation, I strongly encourage you to seek help from a professional Christian counselor, who can help you walk through your crises in a God-honoring way.

Love consists in this: not that we loved God, but that He loved us and sent His Son to be the propitiation for our sins.
1 John 4:10

Women hold incredible power over men (husbands, sons, and even fathers). What we say to them or about them can build them up or tear them down, encourage, or exasperate. This power goes beyond what we say, and into how and where we say it. That is our subject for today.

Lightbulb

We can disrespect our men by the way we speak to them or the way we talk about them.

He Hears What We Might Not Be Saying

I was surprised to discover that men are prone to hear disrespect, disappointment, and personal attacks in what, for us, are innocent communications of fact. Some things just push a man's buttons. What we understand to be a simple reminder can be interpreted as nagging or an accusation of laziness or mistrust. One man I interviewed said, "Inherent in her reminder is a statement of disappointment. For me as a man, that is saying that I failed. I hate to fail. It's not the statement that bothers me; it's the implications of the statements." In my interviews, a number of men said something similar. I had to reassure them over and over that their wives probably didn't mean to disrespect them. They were likely just clueless.

For example, one man said, "Sometimes, if something breaks in the house, I want to try to take a crack at it before I call an expert. If my wife says, 'Well, you're really not a fix-it–type person,' I feel so insulted. She's not rude about it or anything, but it's like she doesn't respect me enough to believe that I can figure it out if I put my mind to it, even if it takes me a while."

Spotlight

Let's turn the spotlight on how men may interpret some of the remarks we make. While our example relates to his abilities, the principle has much broader implications.

Go back to the Day 3 "Man and his challenge" chart (p. 21) and focus on the household task portion. Think about comments you have made about your husband's abilities around the house, and write them here.

_____

_____

What are some ways he might interpret your comments?

_____

_____

Our Words Sink In Deeply

The truth is that, while our men put up a strong front, the male ego is one of the most fragile things on the planet. Our words sink in deeply—not only the words we say in private, but especially what we say about them or to them in public.

Check any comments you have made about your husband in front of family or friends.

❏ He is never on time.

❏ He leaves his clothes all over the floor.

❏ He can't fix anything.

❏ He's a couch potato.

❏ He is always losing things.

❏ He's overweight (or too skinny) or too short (or too tall).

❏ He can't boil water.

❏ Other: _____

Many of us have wondered why our men—who normally have a great sense of humor—get so upset by a little public joking at their expense. Dozens of men told me how painful it is when their wives criticize them in public, put them down, or even question their judgment in front of others. Even good-natured teasing, not to mention more pointed jabs, can be humiliating,

We women often think of this as male pride—but it isn't. At stake are his secret feelings of inadequacy as a man, which we'll talk even more about next week. There's a big difference between feeling prideful and feeling adequate. What happens in public is not that his "inflated" pride is brought down to earth, but that something makes him feel inadequate and humiliated as a man.

In Job 29 (on Day 1) we read what it was like for Job to feel respected and admired. In chapter 30 we see how Job felt after his trials and tribulations had become public fare.

Open your Bible to Job 30:9-15. How was Job mocked by the sons of some men he knew?

_____

Now I'm the butt of their jokes.
Job 30:1, The Message

Now I know you would never intentionally make fun of your man. But that could be what he is feeling.

But now men who are younger than I make fun of me.
Job 30:1, NCV

Read the two translations of Job 30:1 in the margin. What pained Job the most?

_____

Now I am mocked by their songs; I have become an object of scorn to them.
Job 30:9, HCSB

In the margin are two translations of Job 30:9. Circle the words that show how people's words had left Job feeling.

The verbal jabs left Job feeling scorned and ridiculed. He knew he did not deserve what people were saying about him. After all, he was an innocent man whom God was testing (see Job 1:8-12).

Now they make fun of me with songs; my name is a joke among them.
Job 30:9, NCV

In the same way, you may not think you are making fun of your man. A little joking is all in fun since everyone gets a good laugh, right? Plus, our society leads us to think that this is just the way people talk. "He knows I love him," you coo. "It doesn't mean anything."

According to Proverbs 26:18-19, what can a joke feel like to the one who is the butt of it?

_____

Those "deadly arrows" are falling right into your man's heart. And when he is around to hear them, those cute remarks and little asides are hitting your man in the pit of his stomach. For Job then, and perhaps your man now, his sense of manhood was affected.

According to Job 30:15, what did Job feel he had lost?

_____

The trials were bad enough, but the mocking from those around him, even insignificant people, left Job shattered. His very honor as a man was shaken. He felt attacked by the opinions of others. Job had no safe place.

To Tear Down or Build Up?

It is amazing how often we talk negatively about our men behind their backs. Think about the last time you were with a group of your friends and the subject of husbands came up.

According to Proverbs 26:22, those tidbits of conversation we throw out about our husbands (otherwise unpleasantly called gossip) are like what?

_____

We seem to "gobble up" this sort of talk like tasty morsels. Complimenting our man seems almost offensive. Interestingly, the effects are much the same even when the man is not present: The woman's disrespect of her husband becomes even more deeply embedded as she harps on it, and those in listening range may begin to feel the same way.

When you regularly make disparaging comments about your man, it can feed any nagging dissatisfaction with your relationship—a dissatisfaction that then affects him.

What can our words disguise, according to Proverbs 26:23?

_____

What appears to be one way may actually reveal something more serious. Is it possible you are covering up some hurt feelings with your witty quips about him? Are some trademark jokes really digs because you are disappointed in a particular behavior?

Check statements that might reflect possible reasons you make light of your man.
- ❑ I protect my self image by making light of my husband's quirks.
- ❑ I'm not dumb. I see his problems. Here they are just so you know I'm aware of them.
- ❑ Look at what I have to put up with.
- ❑ See what sacrifices I have to make day in and day out because of the way he is.
- ❑ If I am always praising him, he will get a big head.

Stop right now and pray. Ask God to open your eyes if this is a problem area for you. Realize that by building up your man, you are not tearing yourself down. Rather you are showing him the respect God says is his due (Eph. 5:33), as well as revealing Christlikeness yourself.

So What Do I Do?

I can almost hear you thinking, *Wow, do I have to walk on eggshells all the time around this man?* Consider for a moment: Do you want him to publicly tease you about gaining ten pounds? About taking so long to fix your hair? So maybe you want him to "walk on eggshells" or adjust to your sensitivities just as he wants you to honor and acknowledge his.

It's all about loving each other in the way the other person needs to be loved. Even as we help our husbands understand that we have a learning curve on this, we should make every effort to filter our words through a disrespect meter before they ever pass our lips.

Read Proverbs 27:2. What should a person not do for himself?

_____

What should others do for a person?

_____

Let another praise you, and not your own mouth—a stranger, and not your own lips.
Proverbs 27:2

No one likes someone who boasts about himself or herself. Today we might say, "Don't toot your own horn." So if your man is not supposed to "toot his own horn," who gets the job? That's right! You should be your husband's cheerleader. Just as your man will be hurt and angry if you disrespect him in public, so will he think you are the most wonderful woman in the world if you publicly build him up.

I am not talking about artificial flattery. Simply take little opportunities to sincerely praise him or to ask his opinion in front of others. Do you think he's a great father? Tell your dinner guests a story about something he did with the kids yesterday that proves it. Does he really understand the intricacies of growing a great lawn? Bring it up in the conversation. Did he take the kids out and let you sleep in Saturday morning? Tell your book club and make the other girls jealous.

Searchlight

This part of our study is a little longer today. I want to help you get started giving the verbal respect your man's fragile ego needs. For your Weekly Challenge, you have been practicing not saying anything negative to or about your man this week. Is it harder than you thought it would be? Does the negative come to mind more than you imagined? Here are two actions that might help.

Step 1: Get the negative out of the way.
When the religious leaders brought the woman caught in adultery to Jesus, He asked that the one who was without sin cast the first stone (see John 8:1-11). You already know your faults that your husband could joke about. Now look back at characteristics of your man that you most criticize or joke about (Day 4 checklist, p. 25).

Pray and ask God to help you be more understanding about the areas or behaviors that drive you crazy. Ask Him to help you not to be so concerned with each one. As you name each characteristic or behavior in prayer, write it down here and then draw a line through it. As you do, you symbolically eliminate it from your thinking.

_____

_____

_____

*Finally brothers,
whatever is true,
whatever is honorable,
whatever is just,
whatever is pure,
whatever is lovely,
whatever is
commendable—
if there is any moral
excellence and if there is
any praise—dwell
on these things.
Philippians 4:8*

Step 2: Find the positive.

Now we need to replace the negative thoughts with some positives. There are plenty from which to choose!

Read Philippians 4:8 in the margin. On the lines provided, write at least one thing about your man that fits each category. For example, it may be "commendable" that he is willing to work two jobs to support your family.

True _____

Honorable _____

Just _____

Pure _____

Lovely_____

Commendable _____

Moral Excellence _____

Now there is a list you can work with and put into practice! When your man hears you saying a few of these positives, he will feel so adored.

*Do what you have
learned and received
and heard and seen
in me, and the God of
peace will be with you.
Philippians 4:9*

Now read Philippians 4:9. What is the promise we receive when we put into practice dwelling on the positives?

_____

What fantastic news! You can look forward to God's peaceful presence as you do what He expects. You're going to be able to see your man almost literally "light up" as he blossoms from your support and encouragement.

Talk to God. Thank Him for the insights He has given you today. Ask for the Holy Spirit's guidance as you commit to build up your man with your words by putting away the negative and dwelling on the positive.

You have discovered that men often hear something that we did not mean in what we say. Unfortunately, in one area men have every right to read something into what we say—and that is when we jump to negative conclusions about them. When we really examine our communication, we will be astounded by how often it assumes something bad about the man we love. The next element about the inner lives of men shouldn't surprise you.

Lightbulb

A man needs his wife or girlfriend to assume the best about him.

You know the saying "Behind every good man is a great woman"? Well, one of the men I talked to assured me this truism is on target. He went on to say, "If a man's wife is supportive and believes in him, he can conquer the world—or at least his little corner of it."

Seeing the World Through His Eyes

The unique way in which a man approaches the world makes his inner, home-fired feelings of personal adequacy absolutely foundational to everything else.

Read Ecclesiastes 4:9-10. Choose the sentences that best communicate what these verses teach.

- ❏ Two get more work done.
- ❏ It is better to just look out for yourself.
- ❏ If one gets discouraged, the other can encourage him.
- ❏ Each one should be able to stand on his own.
- ❏ Two people working together strengthen each other.

Who did Solomon, the writer of Ecclesiastes, say is to be pitied?

_____

Two are better than one because they have a good reward for their efforts. For if either falls, his companion can lift him up; but pity the one who falls without another to lift him up.
Ecclesiastes 4:9-10

Solomon, in all of his wisdom, reminded us that it is so much better to have someone at our side to build us up—just as God planned it. Remember our role as helpmate? (See Gen. 2:18.) You are the "picker-upper."

It makes sense then that if what you communicate to your man reveals negative assumptions about him, he is hearing disrespect. It also stands to reason that if your man is interpreting much of what you say or do as disrespect, then he must be feeling very alone against the world. He may even feel like he has fallen and cannot get up.

Spotlight

What assumptions do you hold about your husband? Are they leading you to put "thoughts into his mind"? You may assign him motives that may not be true. Using the chart on the next page, let's see how it might work.

Read the woman's comment or question, and put an *A* beside her assumption behind the comment and an *R* beside his possible inner reaction.

1. Have you changed the furnace filter yet?

    ___ He needs to be reminded because he either is incapable of remembering or needs my prodding to do the job.

    ___ She doesn't trust me to do the job.

    Better Thoughts:

2. Why don't you help the children with their baths?

    ___ He's choosing not to help while I do it all.

    ___ How am I supposed to read her mind?

    Better Thoughts:

3. He never wants to do anything fun.

    ___ Every time I suggest something she shoots it down like I am a moron.

    ___ He doesn't want to spend time with me.

    Better Thoughts:

How did you fare? After you read "So What Do I Do?" try your hand at writing better thoughts in the space provided.

So What Do I Do?

The next time you are tempted to make a negative assumption about your man, hold up these stop signs with three "don'ts." Memorize them; write them down if you need to but learn them. Put them where they will remind you not to say anything based on a negative assumption about your man.

Don't assume he needs reminding.
Don't assume he is just choosing not to help.
Don't assume it is all his fault.

Don't assume he needs reminding.

Trust him to work within his own priorities. Asking a simple question such as "Have you done it yet?" seems innocent to us. But inherent in that question is our assumption that he needs a reminder. He is either incapable of remembering on his own or he needs our prodding. No wonder men hate to be nagged! What they are correctly assuming is that we don't trust them to get the job done.

On the other hand, surprisingly enough, about half of the men surveyed did not look at the reminders as negative; they just did not see the job as having the same priority level as their wives did. Other men mentioned that they often felt they just could not handle one more thing. So procrastinating was just their way of saying, "I'll get to it when I can handle it."

Now what if our thought process was something like this: *I asked him to do it. He hasn't done it. I trust my husband. Therefore, there's a reason he hasn't done it.*

Don't assume he is just choosing not to help.

Consider that he may not see the need for his help, and ask him for it. So you think that asking for help is all you are doing? But does your exasperated tone or glowering face communicate that he sure is a scumbag for not helping you earlier? His thought process may be completely different. He just doesn't see the needs you see.

Now what if our thinking went something like this: *I see a lot to do around the house today. My husband must not see the same things. I will ask him to help in a considerate manner.*

Don't assume it is all his fault.

Could it be that the reactions we get from our men at times are not unloving but instead self-protective? Learn to analyze a situation and be ready to accept your part of the blame. For example, a wife who is constantly critical of her husband may spur him to withdraw from her emotionally. "Men are not stupid," says Dr. Eggerichs. "They are reacting that way because they interpret something as disrespect. Even if sometimes they shouldn't."

Can you think of a past behavior of yours that may have created an environment in which your man feels like Job—that he has no safe place to be himself? Jot those circumstances in the margin.

As simple as it sounds, the remedy is to *assume the best.* Could you begin to think, *Maybe I don't give his suggestions a fair shake. Have I been too down on him?* Just as you can choose to demonstrate respect, so can you choose to give your man the benefit of the doubt.

If You Have Blown It

I hope the lightbulbs have been going off for you this week. However, you may be feeling a little overwhelmed by this time. You might be thinking, *Oh, I can't believe I've been doing that to my man.* OK, you've blown it. Well, we all have. No, we all do.

Again, the solution is simple, though not quick. Acknowledge your fault and ask for forgiveness. According to the guys in my research, it is enough just to say, "I'm sorry I said that. It was disrespectful. I know I can trust you." You may need to demonstrate your trust over and over again, depending on how long previous patterns have been in place. He may need to hear these words quite a few times before he believes you.

A house is built by wisdom, and it is established by understanding; by knowledge the rooms are filled with every precious and beautiful treasure.
Proverbs 24:3-4

Getting Down to Business

This proverb is a perfect explanation for what you will be doing during our weeks of study.

From Proverbs 24:3-4 circle words to indicate some things you are learning.

I hope you feel that you are gaining some knowledge, understanding, wisdom, and "good sense" (CEV) as you look at the inner lives of men. I pray that your relationship—like the home in these verses—is being filled with "rare and beautiful treasures" (NIV). Your goal will require some work. But remember, you are not alone.

[1]Remind them to be submissive to rulers and authorities, to obey, to be ready for every good work, [2]to slander no one, to avoid fighting, and to be kind, always showing gentleness to all people. [3]For we too were once foolish, disobedient, deceived, captives of various passions and pleasures, living in malice and envy, hateful, detesting one another.
Titus 3:1-3

Read Titus 3:1-3. What has God shown you this week that needs changing? I have been encouraged to take these positive actions (v. 2):

_____

_____

I have been challenged to change these things (v. 3):

_____

_____

But when the goodness and love for man appeared from God our Savior, He saved us —not by works of righteousness that we had done, but according to His mercy, through the washing of regeneration and renewal by the Holy Spirit.
Titus 3:4-5

According to Titus 3:4-5, God has poured out His love on us because of His

goodness and _____ . God has given us new life in His Spirit

according to His mercy, not by any _____ ___ _____

that we have done.

Because you are loved and because God has been merciful with you, knowing that you have no works of righteousness to offer, you can love and be merciful to your man, even when he doesn't deserve it. Because God doesn't look at what you deserve, you can give your man the benefit of the doubt without feeling walked over or taken advantage of.

Remember this promise: *"This [Spirit] He poured out on us abundantly through Jesus Christ our Savior, so that having been justified by His grace, we may become heirs with the hope of eternal life" (Titus 3:6-7).* Only the Holy Spirit can renew your mind on these matters and help you to no longer conform to the old patterns of disrespect.

Searchlight

Read Titus 3:8 in your Bible to close your study today. Do you believe God? Do you believe that He knows what is best for you, including your relationships with men? He says that husbands need unconditional respect from their wives. Talk to Him about this. Tell Him how you feel.

Are you ready to devote yourself to the "good works" He is revealing to you? Ask Him to help you see the good in all of this for everyone. Thank Him for His incredible mercy and grace.

Your Love Is Not Enough

If you take away only one concept from this study, it should be this one: recognize how _PRIMARY_ and _IMPORTANT_ respect is to a man.

Our men most need to feel that we _RESPECT, TRUST & ADMIRE_ them.

We want to learn to love them in the _____ they need to be loved.

> "To sum up, each one of you is to _LOVE_ his wife as himself,
> and the wife is to _RESPECT_ her husband" (Eph. 5:33, HCSB).

Who must show *agapao* love in a marriage? _HUSBANDS_ .

So what's a woman to do? show *phobeo* respect
Definitions of *phobeo* respect are:
(1) "to be struck with fear, to be seized with alarm when startled by strange sights
   or occurrences, or when struck with amazement"
(2) "to _REVERENCE_ , _VENERATE_ , to treat with _DEFERENCE_ "

> "Nevertheless, each individual among you also is to love his own wife even as himself,
> and the wife must see to it that she respects her husband" (Eph. 5:33, NASB).

Most of us don't know what it _LOOKS_ _LIKE_ to demonstrate unconditional respect.

The wife must _CHOOSE_ to respect her husband in the same way he is to love her.

When you choose to demonstrate respect, they feel _ADORED_ .

Don't
• show disrespect
• tease in public.
• constantly question his judgment and decisions.
The only time a man's guard is down is with the woman he loves. She can _PIERCE_ _HIS_ _HEART_ like nobody else.

Do tell him:
• "I'm so proud of you!" and "I trust you."

By focusing on the good, our thoughts and actions will begin to _CHANGE_

Handwritten margin notes:
ROMANS 12:1-2 RENEW OUR MINDS SO WE CAN LOOK AT THE GOOD.

ANGER = HE FEELS DISRESPECTED

FEELINGS FOLLOW ACTIONS

PHIL. 4:8

week two

The Performance of a Lifetime

Do you ever wish you could read your man's mind? If you could, you might find yourself as surprised as Dr. Beverly Crusher of *Star Trek: The Next Generation*. (OK, I'm a Trekkie.)

Here's the scenario: The confident captain, Jean-Luc Picard, and Dr. Crusher are trying to find their way through unfamiliar territory on an alien planet. Somehow in the process they have gained the ability to hear each other's thoughts.

As the captain leads them toward help, he scans the horizon, points in a certain direction, and, with his usual commanding certainty, gives the order, "This way." Dr. Crusher, who for the first time knows exactly what he is thinking, gasps.

She states in amazement, "You don't really know, do you? You're acting like you know exactly which way to go, but you're only guessing!" Then, with growing amazement, she asks, "Do you do this all the time?"

The captain, giving her a look, answers, "There are times when it is necessary for a captain to give the appearance of confidence."

In the follow-up survey to *For Women Only*, we found that no matter how confident they might look, 70 percent of the men admitted to feeling out of their depth and afraid that it would show. This answer was typical: "I try to perform well and look as competent as possible when inside I sometimes feel insecure and am concerned about others' opinion of me and my abilities."

I discovered from my research and interviews that men seem to be consumed with these thoughts:
- I am always being watched and judged.
- I have no earthly idea how to do this.
- I want to do this.

A man's inner vulnerability about his performance often stems from his conviction that he is being watched and judged at all times. This inner uncertainty leaves even the man who seems most confident dreading the moment when he will be exposed for who he really believes himself to be—an impostor.

To compensate for his insecurity and his feelings of being watched, a man may feel the need to work long hours. Or the constant need to look "on the ball" may wear him down emotionally. One thing is certain: *The idea of thinking he can't cut it is humiliating, which is a feeling a man wants to avoid at all costs.* As a result, he puts up a good front so others will think he is highly competent.

So there you have it. In the spotlight stands a man—maybe your husband, father, or son—feeling certain that if anyone (even his wife, daughter, or mother) really knew him for what he was, they would know the truth—that, at least some of the time, he is not what he appears to be.

As I began to understand this finding, I was saddened to recall that I had sometimes not been very supportive, simply because I didn't realize that my husband could possibly be feeling so insecure. I'm fully confident in Jeff's abilities. Why wouldn't he be?

As you learn this, you may feel sad too, maybe even guilty. Be prepared for this feeling, but don't get bogged down there. We are going to move to what you can do to be supportive of your man once the lightbulb comes on for you.

Lightbulb
Despite their "in control" exterior, men often feel like impostors and insecure that their inadequacies will be discovered.

Weekly Challenge
Affirm your man by finding something good, praiseworthy, honorable, or likable about him each day. Write at least one positive quality in the margin of each day's reading.

Begin with a prayer that God will help you meet this new challenge. Practice every day. Continue to practice behavior and attitude changes from other Weekly Challenges.

I was surprised to learn that men are pretty hard on themselves. One man told me: "We think about what others think about us all the time." Another told me, "Men aren't always as sure of themselves as they look." I am very confident in my husband so I found it hard to believe that he wasn't always sure of himself!

To make matters even more interesting, I discovered that this inner insecurity has a partner associated with it—the feeling of wanting a challenge. So while our men are driven to take on something new and exciting, they are trembling inside, hoping that no one will guess that they don't know what they are doing.

Lightbulb

Men are vulnerable and are driven by a deep sense of insecurity.

He Never Quite Measures Up

Then the eyes of both of them were opened, and they knew they were naked; so they sewed fig leaves together and made loincloths for themselves.
Genesis 3:7

When Adam and Eve disobeyed God in the garden of Eden and sin was introduced into God's perfect world, there was one judgment God didn't have to pronounce (see Gen. 3:6-10). Adam and Eve figured it out by themselves. You can call it by various names. Fear. Shame. Guilt.

According to Genesis 3:7, what was the first thing the couple realized after they disobeyed God? Circle your answers.
a. They were sunburned.
b. The fruit was delicious.
c. They were naked.

What did they do to cover themselves?
a. Ordered online.
b. Sewed fig leaves together.
c. Didn't really worry about it.

So the LORD God called out to the man and said to him, "Where are you?" And he said, "I heard You in the garden, and I was afraid because I was naked, so I hid."
Genesis 3:9-10

Based on Genesis 3:9-10, write what Adam and Eve did when they heard the voice of God after having disobeyed Him.

THEY HID

No one had to tell Adam and Eve to cover up or to hide. No one had to explain that God would be disappointed. No one had to announce that judgment was coming! They already knew that they were no longer the same.

"The ground is cursed because of you. You will eat from it by means of painful labor all the days of your life. It will produce thorns and thistles for you, and you will eat the plants of the field. You will eat bread by the sweat of your brow until you return to the ground, since you were taken from it. For you are dust, and you will return to dust."
Genesis 3:17-19

If Genesis 3:17-19 had been aimed at *you* instead of Adam, how would you feel about the future?

FEAR THE LORD

Just reading these verses makes me feel sad for my husband. Basically, these verses tell us that his future will be a constant struggle, that he will never quite measure up to the challenge. Is it any wonder that he seldom feels he has arrived or has the answers he needs?

In a sense, he feels "naked," and his natural inclination is to "hide." He may do so behind a mask of bravado, long work hours, or even depression or other medical condition. One thing he knows: He is not who everyone thinks he is. He knows his own feelings and thoughts, and he is hiding, baby!

> **Circle the answer that reflects how you think: It is _easy_ / _hard_ for me to imagine that my man feels insecure about anything.**

Am I the only one who was surprised to find that men feel so insecure about themselves and their abilities? Frequently putting up good fronts, they know others often look up to them and expect them to know "how to." It is hard to imagine that they ever feel as though they cannot handle any and every situation.

What Does This Insecurity Look Like?

Let's discover how this inner insecurity—paired with a desire to prove himself—often leads a man to think. Remember, we are not saying this is the right way, just how men seem to be wired.

Spotlight

Recognizing that logic is not always evident in how anyone thinks, put a check mark over the thought bubble that matches the surprising way Fred and Jack may be feeling in each situation.

Fred drove a school transit bus. When no one was on board, he enjoyed going a little faster than he should. One day as he hurtled around a corner, an elderly gentleman shook his head no at him. Fred thought to himself:

> **How dare he judge my driving?**

> **I guess he doesn't need my route today.**

Jack unloaded the big box into the backyard. The kids could hardly wait to see the jungle gym assembled. Jack looked at the instructions and wondered, *Now just what is a Phillips head screwdriver?* Sally came around the corner and asked, "Why don't we call my dad to come over. He'll have it up in no time."

> **I don't care much for tools and stuff. It will be quicker if we call her dad. He'll love it.**

> **This is my Mt. Everest, and I WILL conquer it, even if it takes all day.**

Faulty assumptions (like Fred's thinking he was being chided) combined with an internal realization that they don't always know what they are doing (Jack's challenging project) can create in men the fear that they are just one mess-up away from being "uncovered."

So What Do I Do?

It is a little overwhelming that God has placed us women in the position of helpmate to build our men's spirits. What a huge but wonderful responsibility!

A man's spirit sustains him in sickness, but a crushed spirit who can bear?
Proverbs 18:14, NIV

Read Proverbs 18:14 in the margin. Underline what sustains a man. Circle what it is hard for him to bear.

Your man needs a strong spirit to face the challenges that God has placed at his hand. He needs a place where he can make mistakes in peace and not constantly worry that he is one misstep away from being exposed. If he is feeling disrespected and critiqued at home, he can feel crushed.

Now I realize that most of you do not set out to criticize or judge. You just want him to come home from work earlier so you can spend more time with him or get your to-do list done! At the same time, may I ask you a personal question? Are there times when you do know that what you are about to say will "crush his spirit"? Is your husband ever correct in thinking, *She is judging me. She doesn't think I can do it. Why doesn't she understand that I want to try this?*

Give an example of a time you made your man feel more insecure, not less.

REGULARLY MAKING SUGGESTIONS
WHEN HE HAS DECIDED SOMETHING

Give an example of a time you used an opportunity to affirm him and counteract his secret insecurity.

WHEN HE IS VULNERABLE & DOWN
I ALWAYS TRY TO LIFT HIM UP

Which do you do most often?

UNINTENTIONALLY + UNKNOWING DON'T
PROVIDE THE RESPECT HE NEEDS TO
THRIVE -

If you feel that you affirm him most of the time, great! If you recognize that a lot of what you say may be interpreted as criticism or judgment, then hang in there. You have just taken an important step toward becoming the woman God wants you to be.

As we study together this week, I want to help you understand how you can begin to create a safety zone for your man, who secretly wonders if he knows what on earth he is doing. You are already taking initial steps as you work on your Weekly Challenges (remember, last week you learned not to say anything negative about him to others). Take a moment to write in the margin something good, praiseworthy, honorable, or likable about your man. Using these positive phrases, write a sentence that you could say to your man to support him in this good quality.

[handwritten margin note:] HE IS VERY LOYAL. I LOVE THAT I CAN DEPEND ON YOU AND YOU COME THROUGH. THANK YOU FOR CHOOSING TO DO LIFE WITH ME. I LOVE YOU!

How did he respond when you shared this affirmation with him? How did *you* feel?

HE FELT LOVED · I ENJOYED SEEING HIM FULFILLED + LOVED, BRINGS ME JOY!

As you practice a new way of thinking, you will see some changes in your relationship.

Another Way of Looking at It

We've acknowledged his insecurity and some ways it shows itself. Let me ask you: Does it ever make you uncomfortable to think your husband may not be secure in all of his decision making and abilities to lead your family?

Read Proverbs 18:12 in the margin. What comes before honor?

HUMILITY

Try to be more sensitive to those areas of your man's life about which he feels insecure. Remember, he is a pretty hard judge of himself so he doesn't need you to be even harder on him. Do not consider this need to be a weakness, but a point of humility. He needs you to help build him up.

Pray for your man right now in this regard. Rather than resenting his vulnerability, thank the Lord for it. Ask God to bless your man with humility and to reduce any false pride or fear of being judged.

Before his downfall a man's heart is proud, but before honor comes humility.
Proverbs 18:12

Searchlight

Read again this week's memory verse, Philippians 2:3-4. You have thought about humility for your man; now, think about yourself. Are there areas in which you and your husband compete? Is your need to be right more important than making him feel confident? Are you more concerned about getting things done efficiently than with how your man may be feeling about himself as a good worker or family man?

Ask the Lord to search your heart this week and to reveal to you areas in which you need to be more humble, as well as ways you can look out for your man's interests. Record what He brings to your mind in the space below.

LISTEN, UNDERSTAND, MORE GRATITUDE LESS CRITICISM OR QUESTIONING. WORK TOGETHER MORE ARGUE LESS. LOVE MORE DISAGREE LESS. UNITE NOT DIVIDE.

You might expect that a man's uncertainty about his adequacy usually takes its toll on the job, and that is certainly true, as we'll see today and in Week 3. One man from among the research interviews assured me, "We have incredible anxiety over where we stand at work." If the boss doesn't talk to a guy, he thinks he has been found out. If the boss calls and tells him he wants to talk to him, he thinks he is about to be fired.

However, the male sense of performance anxiety does not, as one man put it, "just end when we walk through the front door." Many men feel just as inadequate at home. In the same way that they worry that they may not know everything about being a good employee, they secretly worry that they don't know how to succeed at being a good husband, father, provider, or handyman.

Lightbulb
A man deals with a great deal of uncertainty about his adequacy both at his job and at home. Today we'll talk about both arenas.

Bluffing His Way Through

The pressure for your man to succeed at his job is real, no matter what his job may be. Getting a job, keeping a job, or getting ahead in a job—all aspects are incredibly draining. Frank Maguire, who helped start Federal Express, takes us inside the unique torture of a man's workplace anxiety in his book *You're the Greatest*.

> Every Friday as he left the FedEx office, Maguire called his good-byes to FedEx founder Fred Smith, and Fred would call back, "Thanks for going the extra mile this week." Maguire always left with a bounce in his step. Then came the Friday when his cheery good-bye was met by silence. Smith then said, "Frank, I want to see you first thing Monday morning."
>
> "I had a lousy weekend," Maguire says. "Not only me, but my wife, my kids, even Thor, the wonder dog. We all had a miserable weekend."
>
> On Monday, when he nervously asked Fred, "What did you want to talk to me about?" he was met with a puzzled look. "Oh, I forget. It wasn't important."[1]

Why do you think Frank had a miserable weekend?

_____

Frank was expecting to be fired. Why would a successful, valued executive at a fast-growing business think that? Why did he assume that a "neutral" comment was a portent of woe? Because inside, Frank felt like an impostor, and he was sure he had just been found out.

A huge, unspoken fear of failure pervades your man's approach to the workplace. Now, one friend reminded me that some men use that fear to get out of bed in the mornings! Fear can propel a man to try what he might not otherwise attempt, but often it's draining. That helped me understand why so many talented, effective men often work such long hours. While long hours sometimes are a necessity of the job, in other cases they are (in the guy's mind) insurance against fear—fear of falling behind or of being cut from the team.

Fearing What "They" (and You) Might Say

Remember our man Job? God decided to let Satan test him by destroying his family and his estate. Even though Job was innocent of wrongdoing (and he declared that in 31:5-6), he still suffered the sting of what others thought about him. We could say he had been "cut from the neighborhood team." His contemporaries saw him as a failure. They were certain he had committed some terrible sin. Surely he was inadequate in the eyes of God for all this to happen to him (see Job 15:1-6).

Let's look at Job again. This time, put yourself in his shoes. Imagine how he must have felt when he knew that everyone around him was thinking he had really messed up.

Read Job 30:9-14 in the margin. Underline the phrases that tell what Job felt others were thinking about him or were doing to him.

Last week, you thought about how Job felt when his peers and family respected him (chap. 29). Here in chapter 30, Job described how others were avoiding him (v. 10), did not hesitate to embarrass him (v. 10), took advantage of him (v. 12), and tried to undo the good he had done (v. 13). Devoting at least two chapters to what others thought about him, the subject must have been important to Job.

Now let's look at another man in the Old Testament: a prince, a man of character, a powerful man in a powerful nation. He lost his temper and killed an Egyptian guard who was tormenting one of his people. Moses went from prince to sheepherder. For the next 40 years, he tended someone else's flocks. In exile in the desert, Moses lived as a stranger in a foreign land, beholden to the kindness of strangers (see Ex. 2:11-25).

Then God began to lay out a plan for him. God wanted Moses to go to Egypt and rescue his people from the oppression of Pharaoh. All God wanted Moses to do was walk in and tell Pharaoh to let his people go! Does Moses remember the respect he once commanded? As a royal-bred leader, does he rise to the occasion? No, but his insecurities sure do.

> *Now I am mocked by their songs; I have become an object of scorn to them. They despise me and keep their distance from me; they do not hesitate to spit in my face. Because God has loosened my bowstring and oppressed me, they have cast off restraint in my presence. The rabble rise up at my right; they trap my feet and construct their siege ramp against me. They tear up my path; they contribute to my destruction, without anyone to help them. They advance as through a gaping breach; they keep rolling in through the ruins.*
>
> Job 30:9-14

Open your Bible to Exodus 3 and 4. Read the following verses and describe the objections Moses raised about what God was asking him to do.

Exodus 3:11 _WHO AM I — UNWORTHY/WORTHLESS_

Exodus 3:13 _BEING SENT — UNCERTAINTY/INSECURE_

Exodus 4:1 _WHAT IF — DOUBT/UNBELIEF_

Exodus 4:10 _I'M NOT — LACK OF CONFIDENCE_

Exodus 4:13 _SEND ANYONE ELSE — UNQUALIFIED_

After all those excuses, Exodus 4:14 should come as no surprise. God was a little upset with this man to whom He had given so much. God knew he was capable of doing the job and was going to see him through, but Moses was a quivering mass of insecurities. His past successes, his natural abilities, even the knowledge that the God of the universe was on his side were not enough to quiet the fear Moses had.

Spotlight

Maybe you think of your man as so confident and in control that he has no insecurities. Your man may not express his insecurities as eloquently as Moses did to God, but it's very likely he feels them.

Look back at the list of Moses' excuses. List some of the areas in which your man also may feel insecure.

WORTHLESS / UNWORTHY / INSECURE / UNCERTAIN / DOUBT / UNBELIEF / WORRY

The fear of man is a snare, but the one who trusts in the LORD is protected.
Proverbs 29:25

Read Proverbs 29:25 in the margin. What always proves to be a snare?

FEAR OF MAN

Look back at the list of your man's insecurities. Does this list include worry about the opinions of others? ☐ yes ☑ no
If not yet listed, are there some areas of his life in which the opinion of others might be an issue?

YES HE WANTS OTHERS CONFIDENCE RESPECT + BELIEF IN HIM

Sometimes things don't go right for your man. People do see him make mistakes. He does goof. And, just as it does for you, failure reinforces his deep feelings of insecurity. When your man feels the shakiest is when he needs the most encouragement from you. He already fears what "they" might say. He shouldn't have to fear your opinion of him as well.

So What Do I Do?

As I researched a fictional male character for my novel *The Lights of Tenth Street*, I expected his inner thoughts to be a lot different from those of my own sweet, Christian husband. Boy, was I surprised when I found out that so many of the things I am sharing with you are true for most men.

Look at Proverbs 29:25 again. According to this verse, who is declared safe?

THE ONE WHO TRUSTS IN THE LORD.

We know that the man who trusts in the Lord is safe. However, a wife who desires to support her husband in this area needs to recognize that, at times, he doesn't *feel* protected. One of my most interesting discoveries about the existence of this struggle is that it doesn't matter if the man has a personal relationship with the Lord or not. Now, don't get me wrong; a Christian man will find the strength through the Lord to overcome a great deal and to not sin in his temptations. But struggle? He will.

Even if your husband has a personal relationship with the Lord, he probably still has those nagging feelings of insecurity. He may not be able to share his deepest insecurities with you. But now that you know he has them, whether you can see them or not, pray for him.

Try a prayer like this one:

Lord, help my man not be gripped by a fear of the opinions of others—even my opinion of him. Give him the wisdom to act as You would want him to act in all situations. May he trust You, Lord, with all the decisions he faces. Help me not to judge or criticize him but to encourage him in all aspects of his life.

If your husband is not a Christian, he does not know the love, support, and strength he can draw from God. While you cannot make this decision for him, you can pray for him. As the Holy Spirit leads, find a quiet moment to share with him the verses on page 173 of this workbook.

Searchlight

Are you making choices that show men that unconditional respect that will encourage and build them up? Read 1 Peter 3:1-2 in the margin.

According to verse 2, a Christian wife should live so that her husband sees what in her?

CHASTE & RESPECTFUL BEHAVIOR

It is my prayer that by putting into practice what you are discovering in this study, some of you will see tremendous changes in your relationships. Still others may even win your men to the Lord Jesus by your respectful behavior. What a privilege and responsibility.

I know that I am asking you to look at things from an entirely new perspective. That is why you memorized Romans 12:1-2 last week. I also know it is not easy to change our way of speaking and acting, but God is ready to give us the strength we need. All we have to do is ask Him for it.

[1]*In the same way, you wives, be submissive to your own husbands so that even if any of them are disobedient to the word, they may be won without a word by the behavior of their wives, [2]as they observe your chaste and respectful behavior.*
1 Peter 3:1-2, NASB

A man tends to think of life as a competition and a battle. He can energetically go "duke it out" if he can come home to someone who supports him unconditionally, someone who will wipe his brow and tell him he can do it. If a man knows that his woman admires and believes in him, he gains the confidence to do better in every area of his life. The problem is, how does he know?

Our words and actions can make a huge difference in countering his secret insecurity and enabling him to be the man God intends him to be. I realize that is a quite a load to put on your shoulders so let's get ready for class today, with Affirmation 101.

Lightbulb
When a man is affirmed, he can conquer the world.

Affirmation Is Everything

As one marriage counselor told me, "Affirmation is everything. When a man is affirmed, he can conquer the world. When he is not, he is sapped of his confidence and even his feeling of manhood. And believe me, he *will*, consciously or unconsciously, seek out places where he receives affirmation."

If a man is not convinced that his woman thinks he is the greatest, he will tend to seek affirmation elsewhere. He may spend more hours at work, where he feels alive and on top of his game; or he may spend too much time talking to the admiring female associate. He may immerse himself in watching or playing sports, feeling the thrill of the competitive rush; or he may retreat to his workshop or home office, feeling like he can control things there even if he feels inadequate and clumsy elsewhere.

During my clinical research for *The Lights of Tenth Street,* several experts told me that a chronic lack of affirmation is one reason so many men slip into pornography addiction. For whatever reason, they feel less than a man, so they seek—and find—affirmation in pornography. As one man pointed out in his response to the research interviews, "My wife may be nagging me at home, the kids may be disobedient, and I may be worried about messing up at work; but looking at the woman in that picture makes me feel like a *man.*"

I am not blaming a wife for her husband's poor choice. Yet, know that home is the most important place for a man to be affirmed, and you are his *only* candidate for the job.

What Does Affirmation Look Like?

You can begin to recognize and practice genuine affirmation in your relationships. These characteristics can help you foster this attitude as part of your lifestyle.

Your affirmation must honestly reflect your feelings.
Psychologist and author Willard F. Harley is living proof of the power of admiration. Dr. Harley credits his grandmother's unwavering admiration for continuing his education. He says, "As a small child, I vividly remember her telling me that I was a genius and more talented than anyone in the whole world. … When my grandmother told me she thought I was brilliant, she honestly believed it, and her conviction convinced me." When a high school counselor suggested that Dr. Harley would be better suited for skilled labor than for college, he rejected the idea and went on to college anyway. [2]

Affirmation should celebrate something about who a person is or what he does well.
"You have a great smile." "The kids enjoy it so when you read to them." "I know you will really wow them at the presentation" are some heartfelt examples that can reveal both your affirmation of him as a person and your respect for what he does.

Affirmation is a way to show your appreciation.
A simple thank you for taking out the trash (with a big smile, of course) goes a long way.

Learning to Affirm

Words of affirmation come easily to some while other people have a tougher time coming up with just what to say. Luckily there is a "worksheet" on affirming from God's Word. You have already started work on it.

> *Finally brothers, whatever is true, whatever is honorable, whatever is just, whatever is pure, whatever is lovely, whatever is commendable—if there is any moral excellence and if there is any praise—dwell on these things.*
> Philippians 4:8

Find your list of affirmations from Philippians 4:8 (p. 28). Complete this list if you have not already done so. Add to this list in the space below.

THINK GOOD GOD THOUGHTS - BE
UPLIFTING + POSITIVE

It may take some practice to change your pattern of thinking. For many of us, it is natural to correct and instruct—or to make "suggestions" that our husband hears as instruction! That is not what he needs from you! You can begin to be more affirming by first doing what Philippians 4:8 (KJV) says, to do: "*Think* [italics mine] on these things."

If we focus our attention on what he is doing wrong in the relationship, our words and actions can unwittingly undermine what we most want—for him to do it right. So focus your thoughts on what is right or honorable or pure or commendable in the relationship. You get the idea!

List something your man does right—either at work, church, or home with the family. Add other things you admire about him.

SMART, FUNNY, TALENTED, LOYAL,
GOOD FRIEND, ENCOURAGING

Make a copy of this list. Put it where you will see it everyday and so "think on these things." You may be surprised at the appreciative words that will pop right out of your mouth.

> Dave was messy, disorganized, and sloppy about keeping receipts, which frustrated his wife's efforts to keep the books and house in order. For years Cindy "helped" Dave with his faults. Cindy often e-mailed him about his financial mistakes, and daily she reminded him to pick up after himself.

Put yourself in Dave's shoes. How does he feel around Cindy these days?

MESSY, DISORGANIZED, NEEDING HELP
+ UNDERMINED

Because of her constant "help," Dave soon found himself dreading the sight of his once-cherished bride. One day a friend challenged Cindy to spend five days saying only affirming words to her husband. She began to praise him for his creative mind, his humor, his fathering skills. Guess what? He ate it up. He responded so warmly that Cindy decided to shelve her "Fix Him" hat forever.

What changed for Dave? for Cindy?

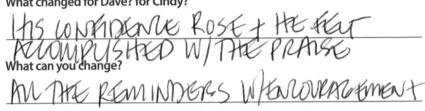

His confidence rose + he felt accomplished w/ the praise

What can you change?

All the reminders w/ encouragement

Now, some of you are thinking, *But he should keep things in order. He was doing things wrong; doesn't Cindy have the right to point them out?* Well, sure she has the right! However, do you want him pointing out your faults all the time? I don't think so! Your encouragement can go much further to strengthen the relationship than your constant monitoring of his "mistakes." You will find affirmation to be easier the more you practice it.

Affirmation Versus Flattery

Check out Proverbs 7 in your own Bible. Have you ever noticed how the adulterous woman seduced the unwitting young man? It was not with sex (OK, not just with sex), but with flattery. *"She threw her arms around him ... and with a brazen look she said, 'I've offered my sacrifices and finished my vows. It's you I was looking for!'"* (Prov. 7:13-15a, NLT).

> *She seduces him with her persistent pleading; she lures with her flattering talk.*
> Proverbs 7:21

Read Proverbs 7:21. What did she use to entice him?

Persistent pleading and
flattering talk

Flattery can be smooth words you use to try to get your way. Flattery is a counterfeit for true admiration and affirmation, which a man is thirsty to hear.

> *But encourage each other daily, while it is still called today, so that none of you is hardened by sin's deception.*
> Hebrews 3:13

Read Hebrews 3:13. According to this verse, what should you do daily?

Encourage each other daily

> *Therefore encourage one another and build each other up as you are already doing.*
> 1 Thessalonians 5:11

First Thessalonians 5:11 says that encouraging one another will

build each other *up*.

Affirmation is more than flattery; affirmation reaches down to a person's core, grabs something of value, and builds it up. And Hebrews 3:13 tells us we should seek to build each other up in this way so we won't be led astray by sin's deception. Your man needs your affirmation so he won't have to look for it elsewhere. He needs you to encourage him so he will not be swayed by the lies of his own insecurities.

Choose two of the items on your list of things your man does right. In the margin write words you could say to encourage him in these areas.

Affirmation Appreciates

One of the most dismaying research discoveries was that only 1 man in 4, or 25 percent, felt actively appreciated by his family. The information showed that men between the ages of 36 and 55 felt least appreciated. That is the time when they are usually working the hardest to provide for their families!

I am sure we do appreciate them, but we just don't realize how little we are showing it or communicating it in the way he needs! Would you be surprised by the level of appreciation your husband feels?

Think back over the past week around your house. Would you say that your man has experienced a sense of being securely and consistently appreciated?
❑ yes ☑ no
What expressions of appreciation did he receive last week?

DEPENDABLE — CAN COUNT ON HIM
GREAT W/ RESEARCH ON CARS —
AWESOME LESSON W/ YOUTH

Describe any areas in which your man might feel underappreciated.

FINANCIALLY — STABLE WORK
PROVIDING — PHYSICAL BACK PAIN
PHYSICAL LABOR

Many men shared with me that at least at work they have a gauge to know how they are doing. At home, they are not so sure. On the home front, men judge themselves and feel that others also judge them based on the happiness and respect of their wives. Even the simplest words of appreciation will translate into a sense of security for your man.

Searchlight

Read Romans 12:9-10 in the margin. As you work on changing your patterns of thought and actions, ask God to help you. Is the Holy Spirit speaking to you about any of the phrases in these verses? Do you need more help in one area than another?

Ask for wisdom as you affirm your man without wanting to manipulate him. Ask for the knowledge to find the good in him. Ask for the power to affirm him with honest affection. Ask God to remind you to show your man unconditional honor.

RELIABLE
SMART
GREAT
RESEARCHER
TRUST
LOYAL
DEPENDABLE
GOOD
COOK
PERSONABLE

Love must be without hypocrisy. Detest evil; cling to what is good. Show family affection to one another with brotherly love. Outdo one another in showing honor.
Romans 12:9-10

The adage "His home is his haven" may seem antiquated and unnecessary these days. In fact, as the workplace has gotten more harsh and less loyal, more demanding and less tolerant of mistakes, I would say it's even more important that a man's home be his haven.

Most of the men I talked with crave a retreat from the daily pressure of always having to perform. Men have told me, "I can be having a really bad day. Things can be going very badly. When I come home and my wife supports me, then I feel like a million bucks."

Lightbulb
Men need a safety zone.

Be a Helpmate

Remember our friend Job? He lost his wealth, his home, his children, and his health. Through it all, Job chose to remain loyal to God.

His wife said to him, "Do you still retain your integrity? Curse God and die!" Job 2:9

His wife, however, had had enough. After all, she, too, had lost everything that Job had lost. The consequences of whatever was going on in his life were affecting her as well.

According to Job 2:9, what was her advice to her husband?

CRITICISM

Did she respect Job's stand? Affirm his innocence? Support him in his time of grief? I don't think so. She ripped into him with, "Let's get this over with! Curse God and die!" She might as well have added the words "you fool." Poor Job. In the midst of all of his losses, he also lost the helpmate God had created for him.

Your beauty should not consist of outward things [like] elaborate hairstyles and the wearing of gold ornaments or fine clothes; instead, [it should consist of] the hidden person of the heart with the imperishable quality of a gentle and quiet spirit, which is very valuable in God's eyes. 1 Peter 3:3-4

In the book *Love Life for Every Married Couple* Dr. Ed Wheat suggests that a wife can gain insight into her role by studying 1 Peter 3:1-9. You looked at verses 1 and 2 on Day 2 of this week. Now read 1 Peter 3:3-6 in your Bible.

According to verse 4, what quality did Peter say was attractive in wives?

A GENTLE AND QUIET SPIRIT

Taking this idea further, the wife who studies this passage "will find that God has designed her to be a responder to her husband's love; one prepared to help, who can gracefully adapt to her husband's calling in life; who possesses the beauty of a gentle, quiet spirit as she respects and affirms her husband; and who continues to delight him all through his life. This is what he needs from her."[3]

Are some of you rolling your eyes? I can hear some of you saying, "I work just as hard as he does." I am sure it is true, but we aren't talking about how you can divide household chores and who spends more hours on the job. Instead, we are looking at fundamental needs, and, no matter your situation, one of your husband's basic needs is to feel supported and cared for by you. Even if in your household that care means that you regularly hand him your admiration instead of a home-cooked meal, I'm quite sure if you asked him which was more important, it would be no contest!

Think of your man's life somewhat like a boxing ring. The boxer goes out into the ring. He is watched by the crowd and critiqued by the referee and the judges. He jabs and he dodges and he sometimes misses the punch; but when the bell rings, he knows that someone is in his corner to take care of his wounds and to give him the encouragement he needs for the next round. That "someone" is you!

> It has been a bad week for Matt. His construction project has gotten behind because of him. His suggestion for modifications to the window frames didn't work out and ended up costing his men two days' work. He will have to work on Saturday and that means missing Jonathan's soccer game. Matt puts his head on the steering wheel as he thinks, *What a loser. I've blown it at work and at home, too.*

Matt's wife, Liz, has several choices in how she might respond to this situation. She can take a deep breath and, in frustration, say something like: "I'll explain it to Jonathan—again! He'll be expecting it. Why can't you just do things the way you always do instead of trying to come up with some 'brilliant' new way?"

Put yourself in Matt's shoes. He already feels bad; how do you think he would feel now, if he heard these words from Liz? What would your husband likely be thinking if he heard these words from you?

THAT HE IS UNRELIABLE - A LOSER

Another option for Liz is to give Matt a big hug and say something like: "Don't worry about the game, hon. I'll explain it to Jonathan. He knows your men are counting on you. You are so good at figuring out efficient ways to do things. I am sure you will make up this time with Jonathan."

What difference would it make to Matt (or to your husband) to hear these words instead?

THE WORLD OF DIFFERENCE

We know our men are human. Why do we often react with surprise when they mess up? We mess up too! What kind of caring, supportive response do we want when the bottom falls out for us? One husband pleaded, "I want my wife to know and understand my weaknesses, failings, shortcomings, and still want me. I need her to be my number one source of encouragement to become the man God created me to be."

Are you in your man's corner? When he's unsure of his footwork, are you giving him that affirming word? When he's been down for the count, do you build him up?

Spotlight

Think of a time in your man's life when he hit bottom. Nothing was going right. Perhaps he made a decision that brought hard consequences on the family. I am quite sure that you remember how you felt. Now I want you to put yourself in *his* shoes.

What was he was worried about? How do you think he felt deep inside?

HE FELT BAD, ALONE, LIKE A FAILURE

How did you respond to him in this situation?

NOT CORRECT - IN SUGGESTING IT ISNT ENCOURAGING + BUILDING

SAFE ENVIRONMENT

Let's think about the ramifications of how we respond to his mistakes day-to-day. You now know that men need to come home to a totally accepting environment where they can safely take their gloves off. Most of us want our men to be able to relax and to truly open themselves up to us. At the same time, I hope you now see that it is up to us to create the intimate, safe environment that makes such openness possible.

Gift Him with Confidence

Despite their veneer of confidence, our husbands really do crave our affirmation. They need to know that we believe in them. Creating a safe place means building up your man's inner confidence. It is about sending the man we love into the world every day, energized by our belief that he can slay dragons.

Sometimes people give gifts to dignitaries or other influential leaders , which subsequently opens doors in that relationship (see Prov. 18:16). In the same way, think of the respect, support, and affirmation that you are giving as a gift to your man. By "gifting" your man with the respect and affirmation he needs, the doors to his friendship, admiration, and influence will be opened to you. You will be brought face-to-face with a strong, confident man.

Spotlight

In what areas does your man need a gift of confidence—as a father, a neighbor, a son to elderly parents, a lover? Write four areas in which you can let your husband know that he is doing a great job.

> *ACCOUNTABLE — LOYAL —*
> *CAN COUNT ON HIM TO BE THERE*
> *GROWING — FAITHFUL TO. ME & GOD.*

Dr. Willard Harley writes in *His Needs, Her Needs* that "biographies of great men prove it, and lives of all men show it: A man simply thrives on a woman's admiration. To a great extent men owe gratitude to their wives for this kind of emotional support, for without it, their confidence—the major source of their success—erodes and eventually crumbles."[4]

> Lucinda's husband lost his job due to a company downsizing. After two months, he became discouraged with the job-hunting game. It upset Lucinda to see him lie on the couch day after day. She hated that he was upset, but he needed to pull himself together and go get a job.

Check comments Lucinda might offer that would gift her man with confidence.
☑ "You have always been good working with people. Have you thought about … ?"
❑ "I know it's hard right now. You have always found a way through our problems."
❑ "The house payment is due on Monday. What are you doing about it?"
☑ "I have always admired the way you can see the light at the end of the tunnel. I know you will find it this time too."
☑ "God has given you great gifts, which I see clearly. An employer will see them too."

Look back at Dr. Harley's quote that precedes Lucinda's case study. He affirms what we are discovering as well: A wife's confidence is a major source of her husband's success.

Does Lucinda's husband have confidence in himself?   ❑ yes ☑ no
Does a man with no confidence in himself have what he needs internally to "pull himself together"?   ❑ yes ☑ no

As the helpmate God has placed in his life, you can choose to gift your man with confidence—and experience the joy of seeing him become the man you want him to be and that God created him to be. You will see him come to life in ways you have never before seen or perhaps even dreamed possible.

Encourage Him in the Bedroom

Those of you who are married knew this was coming. In the husband-wife relationship, the importance of intimacy cannot be overstated. As one man said, "A great sex life can overcome a multitude of impostor messages from the world." Another man sent an e-mail that expressed, "Sex plays a huuuuuuuge role in a man's self-confidence."

I have had scores of women tell me that they have a hard time respecting and affirming their husbands because they just are not doing what husbands should do. Like Lucinda's husband, these men have suffered a slump with no energy and drive left and, consequently, are hard to live with. I always ask these ladies one question: Are you affirming your husband sexually? The answer is *always* no.

We will talk more about sexual intimacy in Week 4. For today, I need you to hear that when you reject your man sexually, it feeds the impostor syndrome whereas affirming him this way gives him great confidence.

His Home, a Haven

For the most part, men are trying hard to succeed for their wives and families. In that daily struggle, you now know that what they need is a quiet, safe place to which they can come home. You know what I picture? Look up Psalm 23:2-3 for my ideas. He needs a green pasture, a quiet stream, and someone who will restore confidence to his soul.

Searchlight

Open your Bible to 1 Peter 3, and see how the Apostle Peter took special care to address husbands and wives. In the adjacent column, direct your focus to some of that instruction.

Circle words in verses 8-11 that would help you to create a safe, encouraging environment for your man. Put a check mark over the ones you feel you are successfully doing. On the lines below, write the ones the Holy Spirit is directing you to work on a little.

_____

_____

_____

_____

Ask the Lord to give you wisdom and energy as you take on at least one of these attitudes to create a safety zone for your man.

Now finally, all of you should be like-minded and sympathetic, should love believers, and be compassionate and humble, not paying back evil for evil or insult for insult but, on the contrary, giving a blessing, since you were called for this, so that you can inherit a blessing.

For the one who wants to love life and to see good days must keep his tongue from evil and his lips from speaking deceit, and he must turn away from evil and do good. He must seek peace and pursue it.
1 Peter 3:8-11

Let me be honest with you. I may have written the book, but it is not always easy for me to be the woman Jeff needs. Some days I have an old-fashioned "pity party." On those days, I have to take a look into my heart and ask, *What is keeping me from putting his needs first?*

Lightbulb

A man needs his wife to be able to put aside her own issues in order to love him in affirming ways.

It May Not Be Easy

Some of you may be having a hard time finding things about your man that you can honestly affirm. You might be having trouble with the entire theme of this book!

Open your Bible to this week's memory verses, Philippians 2:3-4. According to verse 3, with what attitude should you view others?

_____

I want you to look yourself squarely in the eyes and check your level of humility.

Is it hard to find admirable qualities about your man:
Because you are concerned about what he is not doing to meet your needs? ❑ yes ❑ no
Because he is not doing things the way you want him to do them?
❑ yes ❑ no

Feelings and attitudes can stand in the way of a woman's successfully carrying out God's will in her relationship with her man. Some of us find it easier to be "Christian" outside the four walls of our home. Other types of walls go up, however, when we try to change our emotional responses to our man. Is there any attitude or feeling that stands in the way of your affirming the man God has given you? Following are three common issues that often keep us from showing him the support he needs.

Our Fear of Being Walked On

Galatians 5:1 tells us, *"Christ has liberated us into freedom. Therefore stand firm and don't submit again to a yoke of slavery."* Unfortunately some of us take that verse and run with it! Have you ever heard another woman say, "I won't coddle a male ego!" "He's a big boy; why should I have to build him up?" or "I won't be a doormat"? Have any of these statements ever come out of *your* mouth? They reflect a belief in the freedom to express our opinions and a feeling that we need to stand up for ourselves. Perhaps we need to read further.

Galatians 5:13-15 explains that freedom in Christ empowers us to

_____ _____ _____.

Yes, you are free, but don't use that freedom to indulge yourself by insisting that your needs be met—at the expense of what the other person needs. Love your husband as you love yourself. If you want your needs met, then you should desire that his needs be met.

For you are called to freedom, brothers; only don't use this freedom as an opportunity for the flesh, but serve one another through love. For the entire law is fulfilled in one statement: Love your neighbor as yourself. But if you bite and devour one another, watch out, or you will be consumed by one another.
Galatians 5:13-15

> "Why did you hang the picture so high?" Nancy asked. "It is totally off-center. I was hoping we would have it up tonight since the girls are coming over." Richard knew he should never have tried to mark this off his to-do list when she wasn't around to watch him. *Why do I even try?* he wondered.

What do you think is uppermost in Nancy's mind?

_____

When it is most difficult to put someone else's needs first, you can bet that your own needs are getting in the way. Your satisfaction, gratification, acceptance, or security is being threatened. A conscious act of will is required to put your own needs aside in favor of the person who should be most important to you in the world. For many of us women, putting our needs aside may simply mean approaching problems—like an awkwardly hung picture—in a gentler way than we would have otherwise.

But if you bite and devour one another, watch out, or you will be consumed by one another.
Galatians 5:15

Read Galatians 5:15. What will destroy two people?

_____

The scenario with Nancy and Richard could end any number of ways. If Richard shoots back a reply to Nancy, words start to fly and old hurts rise to the surface again. Both people get hurt. If Richard swallows hard and says no more, his defeated feeling of "messing up one more time" eats away at him. He adds another layer to the wall he has built around his emotions and his willingness to help out at home.

Can you think of a time when your feelings and rights got in the way of your considering your man's feelings—either in what you said or in *how* you said it?

_____

_____

Living in the Spirit contrasts dramatically with the "works of the flesh" (see Gal. 5:16-26). Our freedom in Christ means that, because we belong to Him, we have "crucified" the desires of the flesh (see v. 24). We no longer need to worry about exalting ourselves (or about others stepping on us)! If we allow the Holy Spirit to lead us, we will not become conceited, provoking one another (see v. 26). Our blessing will be the very fruit we need to meet our man's needs in the way he needs them to be met.

But the fruit of the Spirit is love, joy, peace, patience, kindness, goodness, faith, gentleness, self-control. Against such things there is no law.
Galatians 5:22-23

Write the fruit of the Spirit as Galatians 5:22-23 identifies them.

_____ _____ _____ _____

_____ _____ _____

_____ _____-_____

After days of learning about what a guy needs, I think the fruit of the Spirit tells us a lot about *how* a man needs to be approached, don't you? If our goal is to stand up for our rights, then we miss the blessing for which we most yearn.

Our Need to Control

The Ephesians 5:33 admonition for wives to "respect your husbands" is a reminder of God's perfect plan in Genesis 2—the order of His creation, with the man shouldering the responsibility of leadership and the woman assuming the role of helpmate to whom the husband gives himself. When Adam and Eve disobeyed God's direction not to eat the fruit in the garden, they were striving against what they knew God wanted. This striving is sin.

The Hebrew word for *desire*, as used in Genesis 3:16, is also used in Genesis 4:7. In this verse, God tells Cain that sin is like an animal crouched at his door wanting to control him. Based on the use of this word, some scholars understand the judgment to Eve (see Gen. 3:16) as referring to a woman's desire to dominate her husband.

Man was created to lead and to provide; but, because of the Fall, this role is not a joy but a burden with which he struggles out of a strong sense of insecurity. The woman was asked to complement and to support; but, because of the Fall, she struggles against that role, torn between her desire to be loved and cared for and her tendency to exert her own will.

> Gail wrings her hands as Mike tries to put their son's new bike together. He turns the parts every way, pushing hard to get some to fit. She knows he's going to bend something. and there will probably be nuts and bolts left over. It would be so much easier if he would just read the directions.
>
> She digs in the box and comes up with the assembly manual. "Here," she says, "Let me read you the instructions so you don't break anything."

What message does Mike hear in his inner core?

_____

Like Gail, many women have a strong need to control things. Or, if we won't admit to that tendency, most of us can confess to being efficiency experts! I think we should learn to forfeit some of our need to control in order to combat our man's insecurity—and, in truth, counteract some of our own unhealthy tendencies.

Which assumption is inherent in Gail's thinking that she knows he is going to bend, break, or lose something?
- ❏ "Mike may be intense, but he's a smart guy. He has good judgment to know how far he can push the bike parts without breaking them."
- ❏ "Mike is not thinking, isn't smart, and doesn't know enough to know when the parts will break."

See what I mean? Obviously, the underlying assumption behind much of our control or efficiency-expert tendencies is not only that we know better, but also that our man is really just a fool. That is definitely an assumption we need to counter with a purposeful choice to trust and affirm—since if we let him, he will usually prove to us that he can do it!

An Unwillingness to Forgive

Does an inability to forgive stand in the way of loving, respecting, and affirming your man? Is it hard to feel kindness and compassion because of his past actions?

> *When I became embittered and my innermost being was wounded, I was a fool and didn't understand; I was an unthinking animal toward You.*
> Psalm 73:21-22

Read Psalm 73:21-22, in which the psalmist described how he had acted toward God. Mark the statement that is true according to this psalm.
- ❏ When I am hurt and bitter, I can do and say things that have no regard for your feelings or needs.
- ❏ Because I have been hurt, it is only fair that I treat you in such a way that you know how wounded I feel.

Actually, both of these statements reflect an unforgiving spirit! No matter whether we are justified or how much we have been hurt, such attitudes tear down relationships. Once again, the Lord comes to our rescue.

> *Therefore, God's chosen ones, holy and loved, put on heartfelt compassion, kindness, humility, gentleness, and patience, accepting one another and forgiving one another if anyone has a complaint against another. Just as the Lord has forgiven you, so also you must [forgive].*
> Colossians 3:12-13

Read Colossians 3:12-13. According to verse 13, what has the Lord done for you?

_____

If you have asked for God's forgiveness in faith, He *has* forgiven you. If God has forgiven you everything and loves you unconditionally, as He promises, is it too much to ask that you extend that forgiveness to your man? The Lord is ready to help you grow in maturity.

Searchlight

Read Colossians 3:12-13 again, looking at the responses God's chosen are to exemplify. Ask the Holy Spirit to reveal the ones you most need to "put on."

I need to (check all that apply):
- ❏ Overlook, at least for now, some of my needs that he is not meeting.
- ❏ Stop questioning his every decision.
- ❏ Speak as kindly to my man as I do to my co-workers.
- ❏ Be more humble about what I think or know.
- ❏ Trust that he's not a fool and usually knows what he's doing.

Do you pray Scripture? When you speak back to God His own words, you can be assured that you are asking for the right thing. You become intimately involved with God's instruction and promises.

Praying Colossians 3:12-13 might sound something like this:

> *Lord, thank You that I am one of Your chosen.*
> *Because You love and forgive me,*
> *I am free to love and forgive others.*
> *Help me to put on compassion for my man's needs,*
> *kindness in my speech, humility in my attitude,*
> *gentleness as I encourage,*
> *and patience as I learn to affirm him.*
> *Help me accept him for the person You have created him to be.*

The Performance of a Lifetime

If indeed our man is not sure what he is doing, then we can look for every conceivable way to _____ _____ ____.

"I'm not sure I know what I am doing" is paired with the sense of always being _____ and _____ and _____ _____.

He needs to know that his wife is in his _____.

When you constantly ask "Why did you …?" he may _____ , "Why did you make that decision, you dodo?" Rephrasing your question can make all the difference.

> **Grow up in the Lord**
> "Now we ask you, brothers, to give recognition to those who labor among you and lead you in the Lord and admonish you, and to esteem them very highly in love because of their work. Be at peace among yourselves. And we exhort you, brothers: warn those who are lazy, comfort the discouraged, help the weak, be patient with everyone. See to it that no one repays evil for evil to anyone, but always pursue what is good for one another and for all"
> *(1 Thess. 5:12-15).*

So what's a woman to do?
"Give recognition to those who labor among you."
Do you say, " _____ _____ , honey, for all you do"?

"Esteem them very highly in love."
Do you esteem him _____ because of who he is and what he does?

"Be at peace among yourselves."
Are you at peace with your man?

"Comfort the discouraged."
Do you comfort your man when he is discouraged and tell him, "I _____ you can do it!"

"Be patient with everyone."
Are you patient with _____ ?

"See that no one repays evil for evil."
Are you careful not to lash out so he thinks you are judging him?

"Always pursue what is good for one another."
Are you always pursuing what is good for him? He needs your _____ .

week three

The World on His Shoulders

Nathan and his wife, Jan, were sitting side-by-side on the couch when I asked him how he felt about a man's need to provide for his family. Without hesitation, Nathan answered, "It is definitely my job to provide financially for my family."

Jan's mouth dropped in shock. Her eyes were wide in surprise as she turned to her husband. "But I've always worked! I've always contributed to the family budget!"

Gently Nathan responded, "Your working or not is irrelevant. Not to the family budget— it does ease some of the financial pressure. But it is irrelevant to my *need* to provide."

Jan was getting a glimpse into another element of the inner lives of men. The surprising truth is that even if you make enough money to support your family's lifestyle, it would make no difference to the mental burden your husband feels to provide.

Nathan's gentle but blunt response was one I heard over and over from men all over the nation. A total of 76 percent of the men we surveyed echoed this same conviction: "I love my wife, but I can't depend on her to provide. That's my job. Period."

Men not only carry this burden but an overwhelming majority carry it constantly. When asked under what circumstances do they think about their responsibility to provide for the family, 71 percent of men said it was *always* or *often* on their minds. There's no respite; the knowledge of their responsibility is always pressing down on them.

This week you will think about how this responsibility must feel for a man—and what it means for you, even if you make a great salary.

The provider element often leaves a man feeling pulled in several directions. He works hard to provide for his family, but that sometimes means taking time away from those he loves. If he loves his job, he is torn. If he is not particularly fond of what he does, work hours can sap his energy and enthusiasm, but he has to keep that paycheck coming in. All the while, he is very conscious of the family's happiness and level of satisfaction with how things seem to be going.

I can assure you that on provider issues men feel deeply misunderstood by the women around them. Whether or not you work outside the home, you may have felt a little confused yourself. This week take a look at where you might fit into this tugging game.

As you prayerfully open God's Word this week, I hope that you will come to appreciate the responsibilities that God has given your husband.

Lightbulb
Even if you personally make enough income to support the family's lifestyle, it would make no difference to the mental burden he feels to provide.

Weekly Challenge
Keep track of the number of times you show appreciation for all that your husband does in the area of provision. What imaginative ways can you find to lighten his "provider burden" a bit? If you are single, evaluate what is important to you in maintaining your pattern of living.

Begin each day with a prayer that God will help you meet a new challenge. Practice every day. Continue to practice changes you are making from other Weekly Challenges.

We have all heard that men want to be providers. They want to club the buffalo over the head and drag it back to the cave to their woman. What few women understand is that this is not just an issue of "wanting to"; rather, it is a burden that presses heavily on them and won't let up. From the core of his being, your man feels compelled to provide.

Lightbulb
At the core of a man's identity is his need to provide for his family

Always My Job
An employee at my local Costco described the provider impulse this way: "It's always in the back of my mind that I need to provide. A man won't feel like a man if he doesn't."

It is safe to say that we don't always understand why God wired any of us the way that He did. As we look again at the Book of Genesis for how He planned and created the world, we can begin to see why a man so deeply feels the responsibility to take care of his family.

No shrub of the field had yet [grown] on the land, and no plant of the field had yet sprouted, for the Lord God had not made it rain on the land, and there was no man to work the ground.
Genesis 2:5

God created man before He created woman. As I understand more and more the responsibility that goes with that honor—frankly, I'm glad that He did. For a minute, let's go back to Genesis 1 and 2. God had a great creation going: light and dark, wet and dry, everything taken care of. The plant kingdom and the animal kingdom were in place, but something was missing.

Read Genesis 2:5 in the margin. According to the last phrase, what was missing?
- ❏ a different sort of mammal
- ❏ a man to be the king of the castle
- ☑ a man to work at taking care of things

Then God said, "Let Us make man in Our image, according to Our likeness. They will rule the fish of the sea, the birds of the sky, the animals, all the earth, and the creatures that crawl on the earth."
Genesis 1:26

Now read Genesis 1:26 and 2:15. In these verses God gives what assignment to man?
- ❏ Don't worry, be happy!
- ☑ Work hard to take care of everything.
- ❏ Relax, enjoy the fruit.

Work and providing are at the core of a man's created identity. He doesn't assume the role of provider. He doesn't do if he feels like it. God has assigned him this task and put this compulsion in his heart. It's not about wanting to be the breadwinner; it's about *having to be!*

The Lord God took the man and placed him in the garden of Eden to work it and watch over it.
Genesis 2:15

As I tallied survey responses, it didn't matter whether the men were married or single, religious or not, old or young—three out of four felt this compulsion. The only major difference was an ethnic one. The compulsion was even stronger among minority groups.

Now, I know that women work hard taking care of things. Our plates are more than full. Some of you might actually be the primary provider for your family. Whether or not you see this need to be the provider played out in the life of your man, it probably is there.

A Job That Never Lets Up

Listen to the rest of my conversation with the man at Costco as we continued to talk about a man's need to provide. "Is the need to provide ever not in the back of your mind?" I asked. "Nope," he declared. "If you're going to be the man, that's just the way it is."

To be honest, the big picture here surprised me as well. Popular culture often portrays men as willing freeloaders. What they really want to do, we're told, is park on the recliner and command the remote. In reality, for most men, the drive to provide is so deeply rooted that almost nothing can relieve their feeling of duty—or desire to do it.

> **Read these Scriptures in your own Bible. Then match the reference with the message that may be driving men about their work.**
>
> Proverbs 6:9-11   No rest for the weary.
> Proverbs 10:4   I can't slack off.
> Proverbs 10:5   I have to stay on top of the game.
> Proverbs 20:13   There is not time to rest.

We women do not fully understand that the burden to provide presses heavily on men and won't let up. As we pointed out in the introduction to this week, a large majority of men (71 percent) say that their responsibility to provide is always or often on their minds. Stop and think about what it must feel like to be conscious of this burden "most of the time"!

Spotlight

If it is true that no matter the earning capacity of the wife, the husband feels the full burden of providing—then look at that responsibility for your family through your husband's eyes. How could he be feeling? What pressures might he be concerned about?

> **Circle the phrase in each pair that you think describes your man's feeling about work most of the time.**
>
> no sweat / (sweating it)
> everything is sewn up / (the seams are unraveling)
> made in the shade / (in the hot spot)
> Other descriptions:
>
> PRESSURE / STRESS / BURDENED

Making it or not, in good times or in bad, men are constantly concerned about the job of provider. Interestingly enough, most men told me that they would not have it any other way. Can you see why? God instilled within them the need to provide, to care for, to WORK. That is what He planned for men to do.

Pray for Your Man

Notice that the Genesis verses you read earlier came before the Fall. A man's need to work and provide were part of a creation that God pronounced "very good" (see Gen. 1:31). Now that you understand the burden a man feels to work and that this responsibility to provide is a gift from God, take a few moments to be thankful. Your Weekly Challenge sets the stage for you to express appreciation to your man. Cultivate this attitude by first expressing gratitude to God.

By the way, how are you doing with the Weekly Challenges? Make an effort each and every day. Changing patterns takes time and practice!

As you consider each of these items, pause and follow the suggestion for prayer.

List here some of the ways your husband has provided for you and your family through the years.

_____

_____

Thank God for providing these abilities or opportunities.

What does your man give up because he devotes himself to his job? Write your thoughts here.

_____

_____

Thank God for giving him a sense of responsibility.

Does your man find purpose and fulfillment in his work? ❑ yes ❑ no
Thank God for these blessings if you answered yes, and ask Him to direct your man's path if you answered no.

Even if you contribute to the financial security of your family, are you thankful for your husband's contribution? ❑ yes ❑ no
Thank God for the contribution your husband makes.

Make praying for your provider husband a daily activity. Keep the focus on him—on what he needs to do his job and on how he is feeling about his responsibilities.

Never as Easy as It Sounds

Even though most men embrace this need to provide and would not have it any other way, we know that God's perfect plan was distorted. As a consequence of the Fall, man was left with a nagging feeling that he never quite measures up.

Do you remember the second element of a man's inner life? Men are insecure and feel like impostors. Now we see how the curse that God pronounced on man affects the inner need to provide.

Once again look at Genesis 3:17-19 for the judgment God gave to man. Circle words that show that taking care of creation will be hard work.

Man taking care of business was God's original plan, but it was not supposed to be so hard. No matter your husband's occupation, I imagine he encounters a lot of "thorns and thistles." Whether he is in an air-conditioned office or literally baking in the sun, it is by the sweat of

"The ground is cursed because of you. You will eat from it by means of painful labor all the days of your life. It will produce thorns and thistles for you, and you will eat the plants of the field. You will eat bread by the sweat of your brow until you return to the ground, since you were taken from it. For you are dust, and you will return to dust."
Genesis 3:17-19

his brow that your man struggles each and every day to conquer the "land" that rises up against him. It is always a struggle and always there. A man can wear himself out. Think of it this way: Men often feel that the security they are seeking for their families is like trying to catch a bird. As soon as you get close enough to touch it, the bird flies away.

What does Proverbs 23:4-5 say about the "wealth" for which a man works? Check all that apply.
- ❏ A man can wear himself out working.
- ❏ The goal of wealth is elusive.
- ❏ A man feels that the security he is working for is always just beyond his grasp.

Imagine the feelings of a man who is having an especially hard time in the workplace. One man, whose business was in a very difficult season, described it to me this way: "Every day, with every step I take, I feel like my skin is being flayed off." Ouch!

Spotlight

What kind of season is your man in professionally? What "thorns or thistles" could he be facing?

A man feels like providing is his job. Even when he likes it that way, the sinful condition of the world doesn't make it easy. As a responsibility that he feels deeply, it also involves deep emotions, as we will continue to see this week.

Searchlight

Read again your memory verse for this week, Colossians 3:14-15, in the margin. The provider issue involves finances, which is one of the most volatile marital issues. The issue of income and who earns it may be a touchy subject at your house. You and your husband may have made or need to make some tough decisions in this area. Perhaps your husband does not appear to be as concerned about providing as you think he should be.

If you are single, be aware of the importance of this issue as you make important household and professional decisions both now and for a future marriage.

For now, will you give God permission to work in your heart? Will you ask Him to show you what you need most? Are you open to learning what your man needs the most from you? Now pray Colossians 3:14-15. Your prayer might resemble mine:

Dear Father,
Help me to put on the perfect bond of unity
in my relationship with my husband,
especially in this area of provisions for our family.
Control my heart with Your peace.
Help me not to worry but guide me instead to be thankful.
Thank You because You are the Provider for all of our needs.

Don't wear yourself out to get rich; stop giving your attention to it. As soon as your eyes fly to it, it disappears, for it makes wings for itself and flies like an eagle to the sky.
Proverbs 23:4-5

Above all, [put on] love —the perfect bond of unity. And let the peace of the Messiah, to which you were also called in one body, control your hearts. Be thankful.
Colossians 3:14-15

Just as women have multiple reasons for doing the things we value, including work, men do too. It turns out that providing is the key arena in which men experience the ongoing risk of failure—when it is the arena in which they most want and need success. Because we tend to see our men as talented and effective, we may not realize how strongly they feel about doing whatever is necessary to protect their jobs and provide for their families.

Lightbulb

A man's internal drive to provide and succeed leaves him vulnerable to a constant risk of failure.

His Need to Succeed

Many men admitted to being driven in their work not only by a desire to provide but also by a powerful internal drive to succeed. Half of the men surveyed agreed that if they worked a lot it was because they felt, "I've got to work a lot to get ahead, and I want to get ahead." Many find pleasure in their work, saying, "I want to be working this much because I enjoy my work."

God blessed them, and God said to them, "Be fruitful, multiply, fill the earth, and subdue it. Rule the fish of the sea, the birds of the sky, and every creature that crawls on the earth."
Genesis 1:28

Read Genesis 1:28. What did God intend for man to do?

BE FRUITFUL & MULTIPLY

God placed man on the earth to be in control, to win over the elements, to increase—not to fail. Nothing is more natural than a man's desire to "get ahead." In most cases, a man finds a huge part of his identity in his work. His creative juices flow there. Your man may find fulfillment in the interaction with others that his job affords. Whatever the hook, he feels that he is making a contribution. Succeeding at his work is all a part of his purpose in being.

In the Book of Exodus, Moses faced the challenge of leading the people of Israel to build the Lord's tabernacle. He had his instructions from God. The people may have wondered how this project was going to turn out, but Moses wasn't worried.

Read Exodus 35:30-35 in your Bible, and indicate some of the skills necessary to build the tabernacle.

WISDOM & UNDERSTANDING

Bezalel, Oholiab, and all the skilled people are to work based on everything the Lord has commanded. The Lord has given them wisdom and understanding to know how to do all the work of constructing the sanctuary.
Exodus 36:1

According to Exodus 36:1 in the margin, how did the men know how to do the necessary work?

LORDS COMMANDED

A man is filled with the desire to succeed at that which God has placed in his heart. Your man may not be a craftsman like Bezalel, but whatever capabilities he brings to his workplace, God has provided them.

Spotlight

What are some God-given talents or abilities that your man feels that he uses in his job? Is he a good communicator? Does he pay attention to detail? Is he talented with his hands? Does he excel at a particular craft?

Can you remember the last time you complimented your man on one of these God-given talents? Write what you could say to praise your man for successfully using this ability in his job.

> MUSICAL - COMMUNICATOR - READING
> BUILDING - INVENTING - ENGINEER

Does your man feel like he has experienced success at work recently? (Do you know?) If you can think of something, write it out and plan to make a positive comment to him about it. If you don't know, plan to ask him how things are going at the job, in such a way that he knows you support him.

> EXECUTING A PLAN TIMELY
> THANK YOU FOR PREPARING OUR OUTFITS
> FOR THE BANQUET.

Along with his need to succeed comes your husband's need to know that you recognize his success and appreciate him. Be grateful if your mate is in the enviable position of loving what he does for a living and succeeding at it. Take a moment to thank God for all the abilities He has given your husband.

The Risk of Failure

In no other area is your man more vulnerable to those feelings of insecurity we talked about last week than in his need to provide. Nothing feels worse than being unable to provide for those he loves—a feeling he wants to avoid at all costs. Men constantly worry about failure at work, layoffs, or a downturn in business. Since a majority of the men (61 percent) said they regularly felt unappreciated at work, it appears that many truly think they are at risk.

We may not see these fears. Our men go off to work everyday, looking confident. However, my many interviews with guys have convinced me those fears are very present.

> A gifted researcher for a notable university, Jake was often called upon to make tough calls in the laboratory. Occasionally he would make a wrong decision, however, and "the big boss" would call him into his office. Jake dreaded these discussions because they always seemed to happen right before his performance reviews. To make matters worse, who were all those sharp, young guys visiting the boss? Should he tell his wife, Julia, that his job could be in jeopardy?

Check the answer that suggests the best way Julia could respond.
- ❏ "Why don't you just confront the boss and ask him directly if he's interviewing those young guys for your job?"
- ❏ "What will we do if you lose this job? Do you have anything to fall back on?"
- ☒ "Baby, let's not worry about this. Let's pray for the peace of God to guide your course. I believe in you and will support you. Always have, and always will."

How would you respond? _____

Day 2 • Worse Than an Infidel

Spotlight

Are you aware of worries that your man has related to his job? Is there a situation he could be seeing as a risk of failure? In the margin, indicate some ways you can encourage him.

I was fascinated to discover that most men feel that they are just one or two mistakes or industry bumps away from losing their jobs. Of course, this fear is even stronger if men love their jobs; the loss of something they love is compounded by the fear of wondering how they will provide for their family.

The truth is, a man doesn't have to lose his job to feel like a failure. His woman's dissatisfaction can be enough to assure him that once again he is the impostor he feels that he is.

The Emotional Turmoil He Faces

In I Timothy 5:8, Paul wrote, *"But if any provide not for his own, and specially for those of his own house, he hath denied the faith, and is worse than an infidel"* (KJV). This verse in the King James Version renders an especially strong impact.

How would you define the word *infidel*?

ONE WHO DOESN'T BELIEVE

An infidel is one who doubts or rejects matters of faith or religious belief. Here Paul was instructing the early Christians on how to live worthy of those who were following Jesus Christ. In that context, nothing was more repulsive than to be an unbeliever. Unbelievers, or infidels, were living under condemnation.

What must it feel like to be a condemned person with no hope?

LOST

In fact, what must it feel like to be even worse off than a person who is condemned with no hope?

DEAD

Both situations are pretty dire, aren't they? Before looking into the inner lives of men, I had always viewed this verse as a warning: If you don't take care of your family, this is what you will be like. Since then, I have come to wonder if perhaps 1 Timothy 5:8 could be seen as reflecting that horrible feeling in the inner core of a man if he can't provide everything he feels his family needs. Could the Apostle Paul have been saying that the man who does not provide for his family *feels* like he is worse than the vilest sinner? Interesting possibility to consider, isn't it?

Although there are exceptions, most men don't need a command to take care of their families; that pressure is already coming from the inside. If the family encounters financial problems, even through no fault of his own, the man suffers emotional torture. A day in the life of Rob can give us insight into that pressure.

Rob sank down onto the couch and rubbed his temples. His thoughts tumbled together. *Could this day get any worse? If Elrod takes his account to another firm I don't know what my boss will do with me. The third installment on Ethan's braces is due next week! What if I lose my job? What did Martha say about Mandy's glasses?*

His misery was interrupted as his family rushed through the front door. Ethan ran to show him his new video game. Martha plopped down the armload of shopping bags beside him on the couch.

"We found some great deals, hon. I couldn't resist. Mandy's growing like a weed and practically needs a whole new wardrobe! How was your day?"

Put yourself in Rob's skin. What emotions are rising up at this moment?

FAILURE — INABILITY TO PROVIDE

Rob felt anger because those shopping bags represented a lack of respect for all he was doing to provide for the family. Because Rob knew things about his job that Martha didn't, he also felt a gut-wrenching horror. He had to take a deep breath before he could answer, "We'll talk about my day later."

Just because some men are not articulate when it comes to describing their feelings doesn't mean they do not experience a wide range of emotions. Maybe your man is very stoic. Perhaps you do not always understand his feelings. Whatever his personality style, know that men experience emotional reactions to their inner fears just as we do.

Martha didn't mean to be insensitive to Rob. She just took advantage of a good sale for a daughter who was outgrowing her clothes. That was a good thing! Just as our emotions are not always rational, a man's may not be either.

One guy put it this way, "About sex, men are utilitarian, and women are emotional. About money, work, or providing, women are utilitarian, but men get emotional!"

So What Do I Do?

Personally, I was amazed at the depth of the emotion attached to the man's role as provider. What lightbulbs are coming on for you?

Choose statements that reflect lightbulb experiences you are having about a man's need to provide. I am realizing that:
- Holding onto his job in order to provide for me is always on his mind.
- If he cannot provide what he feels we need or want, it affects his self-esteem.
- If I make my husband feel as though he is not providing, I am making him feel like a condemned person.
- Even though I have always worked or I make more than he does, the need to provide is built into my man.
- I realize that God has created my man to feel the burden of providing for me.

New insights should bring about new actions! Now choose the new attitudes you want to work on by suggesting some changes in how you act.

Using statement starters (I will acknowledge, I will stop, I will not resent, and so forth), complete an action plan for each insight. I have done one for you.

❑ I realize that holding onto his job in order to provide for me is always on his mind.
My action plan:
I will show my appreciation this week by saying, "Thanks for working so hard for us."

❑ I realize that if my husband cannot provide what he feels we need or want, it affects his self-esteem.
My action plan:
THANK HIM FOR ALL HE DOES

❑ I realize that if I make my man feel as though he is not providing, I am making him feel like a condemned person.
My action plan:
TO THANK HIM FOR ALL HE IS DOING + BE POSITIVE + ENCOURAGING

❑ I realize that even though I have always worked or I make more than he does, the need to provide is built into my man.
My action plan:
MAKE HIM FEEL LIKE WHAT HE IS DOING IS GREAT + THE MORE OPPORTUNITIES ARE ON WAY.

❑ I realize that God has created my man to feel the burden of providing for me.
My action plan:
ACKNOWLEDGE, SUPPORT + ENCOURAGE HIM WHERE HE IS DOING GREAT.

Searchlight

Read Philippians 4:10-14 in your Bible as you conclude today. I love verse 14. While Paul had it together, he still appreciated the support the Philippians provided. More than the physical support, he appreciated their expressions of concern and spirit of sharing. The people had done well by reaching out to him.

Ask God to give you heartfelt concern and a deep understanding for your man's burden to provide. Ask the Lord to strengthen you as you reach out to let him know that you understand his burden.

I must say, understanding more about the inner lives of men has given me a greater compassion for their occasional sense of being caught between a rock and a hard place.

Providing is a man's way of expressing love to his family. At the same time, providing for the family may take him away from those he loves. It takes money to provide and it takes time to make money. If you are like me, you may find yourself complaining that the job that takes so much time is more important to him than they are. How can the poor guy win?

Let's open our eyes and our hearts and see whether any more lightbulbs come on as we look deeper into this element that can be so distressing and confusing to men (and us).

Lightbulb
Providing means more to a man than money to pay the bills.

Providing = Love
Our research pointed out that men and women hold to different views about providing, and our personal experiences often validate those views.

> As Josh and Lorie were on their way home from a party, a conversation that had occurred there was tugging at Josh. Lorie's friend Beverly mentioned that she often wondered if her husband cared more for his new job than he did for her because he spent so many hours away from home. As they pulled into traffic, Josh brought up the subject that had been bothering him all night.
>
> "Lorie, I know I travel a lot. I have to be away from you and the kids so much. Do you ever wonder, like Beverly does, if I love my job more than you?"
>
> Surprised, Lorie paused a moment. "Well … yes. You work so much. I can't help thinking it might mean you don't care as much about me."
>
> Josh was shocked. "Why do you think I work so much? It's *because* I do love and care about you!"

What had Lorie missed? What does Josh feel about his work and about her?

_____

Most men view the sacrifices they make in their jobs as gestures of their love and desire to provide. For a man, bringing home a paycheck is love talk, pure and simple. Like Josh, they are flabbergasted to discover that we would ever doubt their love because of the hours they spend on the job. As one young man told me, "My job is to worry about providing so that my wife doesn't have to. That's one way I show her I love her."

If it is true that your husband is completely aware of what he needs to do to provide for you and your family, how do you think a rebuke affects him? See Proverbs 17:10 in the margin for a clue.

A rebuke cuts into a perceptive person more than a hundred lashes into a fool.
Proverbs 17:10

In a man's mind, going to work every day is saying, "I love you. I care for you. I want to give you what you need." Yet, we often gripe about his work habits, don't we? Translation: We're complaining about his proclamation of love!

Love = Time

Actually, men have a hard time believing that most women would rather have more time with them than more money to spend. Just as Lorie didn't "get it" that Josh's long hours meant he loved her, so is this idea difficult for most men to grasp.

> Matthew was anxious to get home to tell the family his news. A promotion! He was nervous about some of his new responsibilities. It was going to take a lot more of his time but the pay was great. Now they could finish the basement and maybe buy that new car that Sally wanted so badly.
>
> He had hardly gotten the words out of his mouth when Sally flew out of the den, ran straight to the bedroom, and slammed the door. Matthew was dismayed.

Complete this chart for both Matthew and Sally.

What could be going on in Matthew's mind	What could be going on in Sally's mind

Here is what I have seen to be good: it is appropriate to eat, drink, and experience good in all the labor one does under the sun during the few days of his life God has given him, because that is his reward. God has also given riches and wealth to every man, and He has allowed him to enjoy them, take his reward, and rejoice in his labor. This is a gift of God, for he does not often consider the days of his life because God keeps him occupied with the joy of his heart.
Ecclesiastes 5:18-20

Can you see how opposite we are on this subject? As women we have a hard time equating the time they put in at work with their love for us! As you put on this new way of thinking, it can transform your relationship.

Not the Whole Story

Love for their families is not the only reason men spend a lot of time on the job. The challenges of the job, a sense of purpose, and feelings of accomplishment all can light up our men. Respect, affirmation, and success all get rolled into one neat and tidy ball—work.

What does God give to a man, according to Ecclesiastes 5:18-20?

_____

_____

Spotlight

What joy does your husband get out of his work? Does he light up when he talks about it? Is he excited about the contribution he is making? Try to celebrate with him the successes he experiences on the job. Jot any ideas in the margin that would help you help him.

Now, if he works a lot, there does need to be balance. For example, if he is glad to do over-time just so he is not at home, perhaps we need to make sure he is appreciated, desired, and affirmed at home—so he would rather be at home than at work! On the other hand, it is possible that he is caught up in his work because he has a goal of making a lot of money. Money may give him power or a sense of security. One man reminded me that some men feel like they have to earn two salaries—one for now and one for their golden years.

If the rewards that a man experiences from his work are a gift of God, then should we see them as anything less? If his work is this important to who he is as a man, how can it not matter to us as well? Let your man know that you understand how urgent his role of provider is to him and how much you appreciate the burden he bears.

Don't get me wrong—I know I am the last person to advise sitting in silence if you are concerned about your man's time away from family. I tend to go too far in the other direction—as Jeff can attest! But if you put yourself in his shoes and understand how he might feel, he will be more likely to see your concern as supportive rather than antagonistic.

But What If He Isn't Providing in This Way?

Some of you may feel that your man does not fit my description. You are wondering from which planet he landed. Even if he has not chosen to pursue a high-pressure job to make a lot of money does not mean that your husband is not dedicated to his role as provider. Just because he does not express his concern about financial matters does not mean he isn't thinking about them all the time.

He may not be handling things the way you think he should. (Honestly, do you carry out your responsibilities at home or at work exactly like he thinks you should?) The fact that some women feel passionately about the family finances does not remove the burden that *he* feels.

As a family, you may be experiencing a hard season financially. Your man may not be able to provide right now. Our research showed that in situations where men were not fulfilling the role of provider, they became depressed and actually lost their motivation.

> Shortly after their marriage, Tammy's husband suffered a terrible accident. Hit head on by a driver who died at the scene, Charles was severely injured. He would no longer be able to work. Although the accident wasn't his fault, he blamed himself. Charles's personality changed.
>
> Tammy lamented, "The person I fell in love with, the man who was so positive and made me laugh, is gone." Because Charles could not support her, he felt he was useless to Tammy.

If work is a gift that keeps a man from dwelling on his problems, what does he lose if he does not have this gift? (See Eccl. 5:20.)

The j _____ of his h _____

This is an extreme example, but any number of circumstances may leave a man unable to provide for his family. No matter the cause or the façade he puts up, he likely will suffer emotionally if he cannot provide for his family.

So What Do I Do?

Some of you may be realizing the pressure you inadvertently put on your husband by coming home with full shopping bags. Others of you may be grasping just how painful it is for him to earn less than you do. Still others of you may be understanding the stress a man feels when he is pressured to choose between showing his love through provision and showing his love through family time.

The situation you find yourself in does not change your responsibility as helpmate. Once I realized Jeff's provider burden, I grasped that what appeared to be an unwillingness to stand up to his boss wasn't weakness, but a strong desire to be able to continue paying the mortgage! Regardless of what may be happening, understanding where he is coming from as a provider is essential to giving him the support he needs.

But if you have bitter envy and selfish ambition in your heart, don't brag and lie in defiance of the truth. Such wisdom does not come down from above, but is earthly, sensual, demonic. For where envy and selfish ambition exist, there is disorder and every kind of evil.

James 3:14-16

As you grow in understanding, your conduct should begin to change. Are you having trouble focusing on his needs? Letting go of what you feel you need?

Searchlight

Read James 3:14-16 in the margin or in your own Bible. Here James warned his readers that certain attitudes stand in the way of wisdom. They were important enough for James to repeat!

At the bottom of this page, jot down some of the attitudes James identifies that may be keeping *you* from putting your man's needs first, even for a while.

Wisdom from the Lord enables us to do what He expects. Circle words in James 3:17-18 that describe the kind of wisdom that comes from Him. As you honestly look into your heart, which type of wisdom do you most need?

But the wisdom from above is first pure, then peace-loving, gentle, compliant, full of mercy and good fruits, without favoritism and hypocrisy. And the fruit of righteousness is sown in peace by those who make peace.

James 3:17-18

Now, turn James 3:17-18 into a prayer for you and for your husband. Here is how I prayed that prayer.

Dear Heavenly Father,
Fill me with Your wisdom to know how
to meet my man's needs. Thank You for helping me
to understand that You have wired him to be the provider.
Help me to use that understanding to sow righteousness
in his life through my peaceful words and actions.

Every day providers can feel a strange tension between wanting to be depended on and feeling trapped by that responsibility. The vast majority of men who put in long hours do so, not just because they want to get ahead, but also because they believe, "There is no other option." They get frustrated when we don't understand that—particularly when they feel *we* are the source of some of their pressure.

Most men don't need more pressure. They've got that in spades internally. Instead, they need our steadfast belief that they will solve any problems and our steadfast offer to help them do what it takes to stay afloat.

Lightbulb
A man needs his wife to be a part of the solution.

Providers Can Feel Trapped
Men can get really frustrated by what they think their wives expect—but their wives may have no such expectations. Jeff and I have been there and done that! Listen to Jeff's perspective. (He talks more about this in *For Men Only!*)

> Shaunti and I come from different backgrounds. I had known plenty of financial struggles in my life while Shaunti had not. Even though I wanted to pop the question, I had serious concerns about what she would consider a "normal" standard of living and whether I could provide it. Finally, after graduating from law school and taking a job in New York, I figured I could provide.
>
> So we got married and moved into a doorman building in the heart of Manhattan. Doorman buildings in Manhattan are common but pricey. Shaunti preferred one because it made her feel more secure, she said.
>
> *Aha!* I thought, confident in my loving insight into her needs. *Even if I might have preferred a different job, I'm doing what men do. I'm providing security for my wife.*
>
> Then I proceeded to work 80-hour weeks for the next five years to pay for it all. During that time, whenever Shaunti said that I was choosing work over her or that I didn't care about her needs, I experienced a strong and predictable reaction— I got upset. How dare she accuse me of not caring about her when I was "busting my tail" to prove exactly that!

Sitting down and talking about each other's expectations—in a gentle and supportive manner—is essential. When Jeff and I finally came to that point, he found out that the doorman apartment was not nearly as important to me as having more time with him.

When is the last time you and your husband took time to talk about work and family lifestyle issues?

_____

Is this talk overdue?   ❏ yes   ❏ no

To be ready for such a conversation, try to make the effort to understand how your expectations and desires affect your husband. When you are able to put yourself in your husband's shoes (as we've been doing), you are better able to understand how he sometimes can feel trapped by your words, actions, or attitudes.

Become Part of the Solution

Open your Bible to 1 Timothy 6. As we look at a familiar passage about the love of money, start by asking the Lord to open your eyes to anything that needs to be reconsidered in your heart and life. Say aloud the memory verses you have learned so far (Rom. 12:1-2; Phil. 2:3-4; and Col. 3:14-15).

Read I Timothy 6: 6-10. Verse 6 gives us the goal right away—godliness with contentment. How do you define contentment?

_____

Do you see yourself as a contented person? ❑ yes ❑ no

Unger's Bible Dictionary defines *contentment* as "that disposition, through grace, in which one is independent of outward circumstances so as not be moved by envy, anxiety and repining."[1] Another dictionary defines it as "satisfaction with what one has."[2] Sometimes, however, our words and our actions communicate different things, as Janice discovered.

Janice couldn't believe what her grown daughter was telling her. "Mom," she said, "I don't see you as a very contented person."

For more than 30 years, Janice's marriage to a minister had led them to a lot of places, including the mission field for more than 16 years. She had happily found interesting advantages to each place and each home. The Lord always provided just what they needed. She never felt the need to overextend herself financially. Janice felt she fully understood, and lived out what the Apostle Paul identified for himself in Philippians 4:12, "I have learned to be content in any situation."

How could her children see her as someone who was not content?

As though God were making sure she heard what He was trying to teach her, a few days later a discussion with her husband ended with his chiding, "It doesn't matter how much money we have in the bank, it is never enough to you." His words cut her deeply.

Janice never tried to keep up with the neighbors. She was an excellent steward of what God provided. She had always been thrifty and never asked for a lot in the way of clothes or jewelry. She actually enjoyed making do when other women would have gone out and spent money.

How could her husband think that she was not content?

What new ideas related to contentment might Janice consider?

_____

_____

She began to realize that "putting up with," "adjusting to," "sacrificing for," or "being willing to accept" were not the same as expressing satisfaction with what she had. While these are great attitudes we all need to practice at one time or another, our men are ultrasensitive to our levels of satisfaction. If your man senses disappointment from you, he may internalize it as his failure to provide. Even if this feeling is wrong and you are not saying he is a failure, the provider impulse in him leads him (at least sometimes) to suffer as though you were saying otherwise.

What does all this mean for how you communicate? Well, if it is unlikely that your family can afford that Caribbean vacation this year, then begin to get excited about the less expensive excursion. Refrain from sighing about putting this trip aside for a while. Make sure he knows you're excited, not just willing, to stay with friends at the beach in the off-season.

If he's feeling (like many men) that you don't understand the necessity of saving for retirement, perhaps you can say, "Yeah, it would be fun to redecorate the den, but you're right that we need to build up a little more savings first. Let me ask, do you think we could plan for that next spring, if we've got _x_ amount saved?"

First Timothy 6:7 reminds us of what?

_____

You don't need me to tell you that your man is more important than things. Most women choose their man over the stuff, but does _he_ know that? For example, you may need to say, "Sure, it would be fun to redecorate (or have the new XBox game), but we are all much more excited that you've got that more family-friendly job, even if it pays less. The kids and I would much rather have you than a new toy!"

What can you say or do to show your man that he is more important to you than the things he provides?

_____

In our _For Women Only_ research, one interviewee-husband suggested: "Make sure he knows your pleasure in any financial progress so he knows that all his obsessive hard work was worth it. When he comes in really late from an extra long day at the office, surprise him with a thank-you gift. Use your imagination."

What We Want Versus What We Need

Our society bombards us with materialism 24/7. Do we have food? Gratefully, most of us do in abundance, but is it the right brand, and does it come from the best restaurant? Do we have clothing? Sure, but did it come from the most popular store? Distinguishing between what we need and what we want can be difficult.

Read 1 Timothy 6:8. What was enough to bring Paul contentment?

_____

What about you? List two items you wish you owned. Are they wants or needs?

_____

A before-you-buy checklist

Do I have the money to make this purchase?

Am I going contrary to family financial plans with this purchase?

Is this a need or a want?

Is the amount, the size, or the quality a must right now?

Will this purchase put an unnecessary burden on my husband or on me?

Do you ever find yourself unhappy because you don't have some things you want (as opposed to need)? ❑ yes ❑ no
List two things for which you do feel satisfaction.

_____

_____

How can you let your man know that you don't have to have everything you want to be content?

_____

When Jeff and I sat down and talked over our goals for our family, Jeff discovered that he did not have to work 80 hours a week to make me happy. I would have been glad to down-size if it meant having _him_ back. But for guys, the provider drive is so strong that it is hard for them to really believe us sometimes, especially when they see us making choices that require a huge salary. Him or an expensive car? Let him know it is no contest!

According to I Timothy 6:9, chasing after material things can lead a person into what?

_____

Wanting more than we have can lead to dangerous habits, such as taking on too much credit or overextending our budget. Now, wanting to improve ourselves and have quality is not inherently wrong! Please don't hear me saying that, but does the desire for what you cannot have make you dissatisfied with what you can afford or what your man can provide? Ecclesiastes 6:9 tells us, _"Better what the eyes see than wandering desire. This too is futile and a pursuit of the wind."_ If this is an issue, take steps together now so that family spending does not spiral out of control.

Willard Harley in _His Needs, Her Needs_ observes that "many people think they need things they may not really need. They sometimes become their own worst enemies. They sacrifice the fulfillment of their marital need for financial support by creating a standard of living they cannot meet. Men sometimes work themselves to an early grave providing for living standards that their family can do without."[3]

Does your husband feel pressure to provide something you would be just as happy without? ❑ yes ❑ no

How can you let him know?

_____

Paul warns that the love of money, not money itself, is a root of other evils. Putting money first can lead to all sorts of problems.

According to I Timothy 6:10, what happens when people fall in love with money?

_____

Could your husband be feeling "pierced by pain" in his efforts to earn money and in the way the family spends it? ❏ yes ❏ no

Once when we were going through a hard time financially, Jeff asked me to just not let him see me come in the house with shopping bags. While he trusted me to only make the necessary purchases, he just could not handle the sight of the bags!

Spotlight
Are there some simple changes that the two of you could agree on, that could help relieve your husband's pain? Talk about it together.

By the way, we often want to blame the evil of "loving money" if our man is working more than we want. Don't jump to this conclusion without a lot of conversation. First, judge your own heart, and then express your concern to your man.

Are You Getting His Message?
More than anything your man needs to know that you are behind him all the way. Cars, paychecks, and vacations are measurable signs of his love for you. He needs to know you are getting the message. One guy's perspective wraps up what I want you to hear today:
"The burden to provide is so great that when it's eased for a while—even just a little—it feels fantastic. If it can't be lightened, the weight can break the back of the bearer. When the burden is shared, whether emotionally, tangibly (increasing dollars or decreasing lifestyle), or through encouragement, life feels so much lighter and easier. When a man is encouraged, supported, and appreciated—even if he's not Mr. Big Bucks—he feels better as a man."

Searchlight
Is the Lord showing you any changes you need to make this week? Don't let those thoughts get away from you, but jot them in the margin so you can recall them. Read Proverbs 30:7-9 in your Bible, and turn these verses into a prayer.

Lord, give me what I need.
Don't give me so much that I put it before You.
Don't leave me in need so that I turn from You.
Keep me honest, honest with myself and with my man.

Yesterday you took a serious look at your attitudes toward family resources. You discovered that most men are greatly relieved to know that their wives realize that they can spend less and still be happy! That, combined with our emotional support, does wonders for the man's feeling that "we can get through this" together.

How can we be emotionally supportive when *we* need support? Today we will look at both sides of this coin—giving support and receiving support.

Lightbulb
A man needs to be actively appreciated as the provider.

Say It Often

Most of us want to support our men. In the provider issue, this support means understanding them, helping to relieve the pressure they feel rather than adding to it, and consistently showing them appreciation. Most couples have seasons of plenty and seasons of want. One man gave a great summation of what a man needs no matter the financial situation. "Thank him regularly for providing. He forgets quickly." Who knew?

For this reason also, since the day we heard this, we haven't stopped praying for you. We are asking that you may be filled with the knowledge of His will in all wisdom and spiritual understanding, so that you may walk worthy of the Lord, fully pleasing [to Him], bearing fruit in every good work and growing in the knowledge of God.

May you be strengthened with all power, according to His glorious might, for all endurance and patience, with joy giving thanks to the Father, who has enabled you to share in the saints' inheritance in the light.

Colossians 1:9-12

Before this week, when was the last time you simply thanked your man for all he does to provide for you?

_____

Make a list of the things for which you can thank your provider husband.

_____

_____

_____

Write a phrase of thanks that you will share with your man:

" _____

_____

_____ "

Use this phrase soon! Watch his eyes light up as he feels your encouragement.

Spotlight
Lifting your man up in prayer is another way to show gratitude. Take a minute to read Colossians 1:9-12. For what situation can you ask God to fill him with knowledge and wisdom?

What decision is he facing for which he needs power to make a godly choice?

_____

_____

Stop right now and read aloud these verses as a prayer for your husband. Replace the pronoun *you* with his name. Regularly pray this Scripture for him.

What About Me?

As you better understand what is going on inside your man, you often have to make one-sided changes. The one person you can change is you! I have received many e-mails telling me about salvaged relationships because the woman made a decision to meet her husband's inner needs, regardless of any changes he made.

Many of us have faced difficult financial seasons in recent years, and obviously it is hard then to feel a sense of gratitude. I understand that it may be hard for some of you to feel supportive of your man in this provider issue. It is easy to get nervous and want to blame our husbands or pressure them to "do something" differently.

This is one of those sensitive areas in which you need to try to make the decision to support him and show gratitude. Remember a man's need to be respected and affirmed? Because the role of provider is so ingrained in his inner core, he especially needs your trust in this area. I am not saying it is always easy, but there are some actions you can take to make it more doable.

Read Luke 12:22-26 and notice Jesus' first instruction to His disciples: "Don't

_____." According to verses 25-26, how effective is worrying?

_____

Spotlight

How do you think a man feels when he knows his wife is worried about finances? What do you think your husband is feeling?

A man doesn't need added pressure. Those feelings of failure are never far away. He is already suffering while you are asking, "What do I do when I can't see how the bills will be paid or how we will make it in retirement?"

What is Jesus' response and reminder about worry in Luke 12:24?

_____

Having gone through a difficult financial season with my husband, I can say that the answer is to cast our cares for provision on the Lord rather than on our men. In the end, it is His job to carry the burden, even as He directs us. And He promises He will!

Then He said to His disciples: "Therefore I tell you, don't worry about your life, what you will eat; or about the body, what you will wear. For life is more than food and the body more than clothing. Consider the ravens: they don't sow or reap; they don't have a storeroom or a barn; yet God feeds them. Aren't you worth much more than the birds? Can any of you add a cubit to his height by worrying? If then you're not able to do even a little thing, why worry about the rest?"
Luke 12:22-26

Take a Step Back

Regardless of the contribution you make or the practical arrangements of who pays the bills at your house, your man feels the entire burden of providing. Is it hard for you to allow him to shoulder this responsibility? Do you find it hard not to worry? to let go of control? In order to let go, you have to learn to trust God in this area of your life.

During these weeks, you have been reminded that God's way is the best way. Proverbs 3 sets forth some biblical standards that apply beautifully to the provider issue.

My son, don't forget my teaching, but let your heart keep my commands; for they will bring you many days, a full life, and well-being.
Proverbs 3:1-2

The writer of Proverbs 3:1-2 says that doing things God's way will bring what?

_____

God's way is to respect your husband by supporting him as he feels the burden to be the provider.

Never let loyalty and faithfulness leave you. Tie them around your neck; write them on the tablet of your heart.
Proverbs 3:3

According to Proverbs 3:3, with what should you always be concerned?

_____

Are you loyal to the commitments you make to your husband to set spending limits, to save, and to follow the budget?
❏ yes   ❏ no   ❏ well, sometimes

> As Paula loaded her bags into the trunk, Vicki couldn't help but ask, "I thought you and Tom had agreed to only spend $50 on each other this year? Isn't that like the fourth present you've bought him?" Paula slammed the trunk with a chuckle. "Well, you know, it's Christmas! If he only spends $50 on me, he's in trouble!"

What does Paula need to do to remain loyal to her commitment?

_____

Being faithful to your husband means more than honoring your marriage vows sexually. When we lie, hide, sneak, or connive, we are not being faithful. Does he feel that we are being faithful if we are consistently at odds with him about money? Probably not.

Then you will find favor and high regard in the sight of God and man.
Proverbs 3:4

Proverbs 3:4 reminds us that when we follow God's way, then we will find

_____

Getting things our way may not be God's way. It doesn't mean that what we want or need is wrong. It means that the attitude with which we are forcing our way may be contrary to the attitude God says a wife should have.

One woman put it this way: "I don't agree with my husband all the time, but I have to stand with him because he is the one responsible in God's eyes. That is exactly what I tell him.

Sometimes I can't say what I feel because God won't let me. In these situations, God always honors my obedience to Him." Of course, you need to be able to discuss matters of importance with your husband, but the issue here is attitude.

According to Proverbs 3:5, the fundamental attitude we should have is to

_____

Trust in the LORD with all your heart, and do not rely on your own understanding.
Proverbs 3:5

Don't try to figure it out all by yourself! Trust the Lord to provide. Trust Him to guide your husband. (By the way, this is a great Scripture to pray daily for your husband.)

Indicate here some times that your actions convey you are not trusting God.

_____

_____

Proverbs 3:6 tells us what it looks like to trust God. Fill in the blanks to reveal this two-step process:

t_____ _____ _____; let Him g_____ _____

Think about Him in all your ways, and He will guide you on the right paths.
Proverbs 3:6

You may think that you really know best when it comes to providing for your family. Your husband may want you to handle the details because you are better than he is with record keeping, for example. Remember that such an arrangement does not remove from him the burden he feels. If he is already feeling insecure about providing, then he doesn't need you to "have all the answers."

Now read Proverbs 3:7. What is the exhortation here?

_____

Don't consider yourself to be wise; fear the LORD and turn away from evil.
Proverbs 3:7

When you think you are the only one who can be right, then you can be led down a path of evil. When you feel that your rights have been violated or your wisdom ignored, or that something is more important in your man's life than you are, then you can be tempted to respond in ways that are less than productive.

Check any ways you are tempted to respond to him:
❏ seek revenge
❏ get hurt or angry
❏ let him know you are not happy
❏ hold a grudge
❏ become indignant

Spotlight
If you exhibit any of these attitudes, how is your man likely to interpret them? Check one:
❏ Does she think I am just stupid?
❏ She does not trust me to take care of her.
❏ She never tries to understand where I am coming from.

Most men shut down when we get emotional about a subject. We thought it meant they didn't care what we thought. Now you know they are dealing with a wealth of emotions deep in their core.

The solution to this problem can also be found in Proverbs 3:7—*"fear the LORD."* The word for *fear* actually has the meaning of respecting the Lord. For the purposes of our study, we could say, "Respect the way God says it should be done. Respect the way He has created your man. Respect the role He has given you among men—to *help* your man."

Once again God says, in essence: "Follow the instruction manual and it will be OK. Just do it My way and you will receive strength, strength you did not know you even had." You have heard what stress and worry can do to your body; God promises that if we will trust Him, we will even feel better! (See Prov. 3:8.)

Honor the LORD with your possessions and with the first produce of your entire harvest; then your barns will be completely filled, and your vats will overflow with new wine.
Proverbs 3:9-10

Proverbs 3:9-10 tells us to use our possessions to

_____

Are you honoring God with all your "stuff"? Or is it getting in the way? God makes a promise. "Honor me with your possessions, and you will have all you need."

Not everything that you have learned about the inner lives of men has left you rejoicing this week. You are gaining understanding, but that is often accompanied by revelations about yourself that are hard to accept.

Do not despise the LORD's instruction, my son, and do not loathe His discipline; for the LORD disciplines the one He loves, just as a father, the son he delights in.
Proverbs 3:11-12

What does Proverbs 3:11-12 say to you about your habits, attitudes, and actions?

_____

Do not resist His instruction. Give Him permission to clean house and to change the pattern of your life to fit His pattern. God loves you, and He delights in you. He is delighted as He sees you already affirming and supporting your man with the respect he is due. He delights in your humble spirit. His plans for you are the best!

In the awe-inspiring conclusion to the *Lord of the Rings* trilogy, when the hero is completely exhausted from carrying his terrible burden, his best friend lifts him to his shoulders, crying, "I can't carry it for you—but I can carry you!" By praying for our husbands and looking to the Lord rather than to our circumstances, we trust Him to carry both our husband and his burden. Then, from the overflow of our hearts, we can give back and encourage our men.

Searchlight

Close by thinking about Philippians 4:6: *"Don't worry about anything, but in everything, through prayer and petition with thanksgiving, let your requests be made known to God."*

What are you worried about? Turn these worries over to the Lord. Thank Him for the provisions that He is going to make.

The World on His Shoulders

For a man, his drive to provide is a:

💡 _____ **and** _____ **that runs deep.**

Providing is _____ on his mind.

We can make the problem worse by being _____.

Guys run everything through a grid , asking

"Am I _____ _____ for my family?"

💡 **Huge part of his _____.**

It's fun to do well, to get ahead, to be good at what he does.

In essence, many guys expressed: "Our job isn't just part of us, it _____ us!"

💡 **Way to do something _____.**

They want to _____ the world.

💡 _____.

"I can take care of my family!"

💡 **Main way that he says "I _____ you."**

He thinks he has no _____.

The appropriate response is _____, not criticism.

💡 _____.

He will work long hours and do whatever is necessary to NOT be at risk.

Sometimes we send him signals that _____ is more important than him.

So what's a woman to do?

Talk to your husband about the kind of _____ you both want.

_____ your man.

Evaluate signals you are sending and ways you may be pushing his "buttons."

week four

Sex Changes Everything

Women, we are faced with a crisis! Men are worried that we are not even aware of it! *Men aren't getting enough sex.*

I can hear your howls of laughter. It's not exactly groundbreaking news that men want more sex. We know they are sexual creatures. I do think that you are going to be fascinated this week when you realize how strongly they feel this need, and you may be blown away when you understand why.

Our culture portrays sex as a physical need for men. However, as I conducted research around the country, it became clear that the importance of sex had little to do with the physical. In fact, to a husband it was emotional, all about feeling *desired* by his wife. On each survey and in random interviews, this theme emerged with great urgency. Being desired by his wife also gave a man a sense of well-being in other areas of his life.

When men were asked how important it is for them to feel sexually wanted and desired by their wives, an astounding 97 percent said "getting enough sex" wasn't, by itself, enough; they wanted to feel wanted. In the entire survey, this was the question that men most agreed on.

We also gave men this scenario and question: *You are getting all the sex you want, but your wife is reluctant or simply accommodates your needs. Will you be sexually satisfied?* A total of 74 percent said that they still would feel empty if their wives were not engaged and satisfied. A huge signal to a man of whether he is desired and desirable is whether his wife enjoys their intimacy together.

One man I interviewed summed it up this way:

> "Everyone thinks women are more emotional than men [when it comes to sex] … that women are more into the emotion and cuddling of it. So women think there are no emotions there (for the guy)., but there *are,* and when you say no, you are messing with all those emotions."

Sex makes your husband feel loved—in fact, he cannot feel completely loved without it. You have discovered that he often feels isolated and burdened by secret feelings of inadequacy. Making love with you assures him that you find him desirable, salves a deep sense of loneliness, and gives him the strength and well-being necessary to face the world with confidence.

Before we go any further, let me clarify a few things. First, while there continue to be ways in which singles are addressed this week, know that this week focuses *exclusively* on sexual intimacy within the God-ordained marriage relationship. A distinctive Weekly Challenge and daily "If You Are Single" sections do suggest ways this week's study applies to singles.

Second, we will be focusing on the apparent majority of cases, in which the husband tends to crave more sex than he is getting. You should know that according to our surveys of women in *For Men Only* (Multnomah), fully 25 percent of women found themselves in the reverse situation. If you are one of these women, know that many of these truths will still apply; but please recognize that this week, of necessity, focuses on the majority of cases.

Lightbulb

Your sexual desire for your husband profoundly affects his sense of well-being and confidence in all areas of his life.

Weekly Challenge

For married women: This week track the messages you may be sending your husband regarding your desire (or lack thereof) for him. In what ways can you make progress in understanding and meeting the needs of his heart through sexual intimacy?

For single women: Observe how the media portrays a man's view of sex. What messages does it convey about how the culture thinks guys are wired versus how they really are created by God?

Everyone: Begin each day with a prayer that God will help you meet a new challenge. Practice every day. Continue to practice changes you are making from other Weekly Challenges.

How would you feel if your husband stopped talking to you? No comments, no grunts, no nothing. Just silence. For your husband, a lack of sex is just as emotionally wounding as a lack of communication is to you—and just as dangerous to your marriage.

Although popular opinion portrays males as one giant sex gland with no emotions attached, that is the furthest thing from the truth. Because men don't tend to describe their sexual needs in emotional terms, women may not realize that sex has that type of significance to them.

Lightbulb
Sex meets an overwhelming emotional need in a man.

If You Are Single

A man's need for sex is powerful. Arousal of that need does not always wait for a wedding ring. The Bible is clear that sex is designed for those who are married.

Read Song of Songs 3:5 in your Bible. What is the warning here?

_____

As you read this week, pray for your future husband should that be your path. Pray that God will make you the best helpmate for him. Consider the workbook questions from the perspective of how God has created men—and how that may be different from how our culture portrays them. If the Lord has marriage in His plans for you, then you don't want to go into it with the wrong assumptions!

Young women of Jerusalem, I charge you, by the gazelles and the wild does of the field: do not stir up or awaken love until the appropriate time.
Song of Songs 3:5

You Complete Him
Something fundamental in a man's makeup makes sexual intimacy with a desiring partner—his helpmate, his wife—an absolutely overwhelming emotional need. More than just physical bonding, a man's need to be desired by his wife reaches the very core of his being. The Bible calls such a bond "becoming one flesh." When you hear this expression, you may immediately think of the physical act that brings two people together, but it is much more.

Read Genesis 2:18-23 in your Bible. What was the one thing in God's new creation that He considered "not good"?

_____

What did He do about it?

_____

God saw that it was not good for man to be alone. So He created a helper perfectly suited for Adam. He created this helper out of man himself. "God taught us that for man there is no substitute, no alternative plan, no better companion than his wife. The void which originally was caused by taking 'bone of my bone, flesh of my flesh' can be filled only by the presence of woman. Since a part of Adam went to make Eve, a man remains incomplete without his Eve."[1]

In the movie *Jerry Maguire,* Jerry returns to the love of his life, uttering the words, "I love you. You ... complete me." Many in our society today scoff at such an idea. For a culture bent on glorifying the individual, such a sentiment becomes the punch line for a joke. For those of us who understand Genesis 2:18, it is a beautiful line and a foundational understanding.

Based on Genesis 2:24-25, how would you describe the relationship of the first couple? Check all that apply.
❑ innocent ❑ unashamed ❑ open ❑ intimate

This is why a man leaves his father and mother and bonds with his wife, and they become one flesh. Both the man and his wife were naked, yet felt no shame.
Genesis 2:24-25

In their innocence the man and the woman were unashamedly bonded. Their intimacy was so profound and open that, at this moment at least, nothing stood in the way. Ladies, this is the way God designed our relationship with our husbands to be! He thought it was a very good idea! (See Gen. 1:31.)

Man's deep need for his wife is more than physical. His emotional need to bond with his helpmate is a reminder of how we were created. Something is missing in your husband, and only you can fill that void.

When you read the preceding paragraph, how do you feel?

_____

I am thinking, *Wow. What an honor! What a cherished place to hold! Isn't it exciting?* But in all honesty, I am also thinking, *What a responsibility!*

He Needs You to Respond

I asked you a question at the beginning of today's study: How would you feel if your man stopped talking to you?

Check any of these feelings that came to your mind.
❑ abandoned   ❑ something is wrong with me
❑ lonely   ❑ slighted
❑ hurt   ❑ frustrated

Most wives would be devastated if their husbands did not communicate with them. That is how a man feels when his wife does not make him feel desirable. I think many of us women just don't understand the emotional consequences of our sexual response— or lack of one.

Spotlight
One man who participated in my research related this sentiment.: "[Sometimes] A man really does feel isolated, even with his wife. In making love, there is one other person in this world that you can be completely vulnerable with and be totally accepted and nonjudged. It is a solace that goes very deep into the heart of a man."

Now put your husband in the spotlight. Even though you may still find it hard to believe he feels this way, complete the following sentence.

When I am unavailable sexually to my husband, he must feel

_____

One man described his feelings this way: "I wish that my wife understood that making a priority of meeting my intimacy needs is the loudest and clearest way she can say, 'You are more important to me than anything else in the world.' It is a form of communication that speaks more forcefully, with less room for misinterpretation, than any other."

Can't you just hear the heart cries of men? One of the most important emotional needs a man has is to feel that his wife desires him.

Change Your Way of Thinking

At the most basic level, then, your man wants *to be desired*. As one survey-taker explained, "I think that my wife, after 20-some years of marriage, knows how important my need for sex is, but I wish she knew how important it is to me that she *needs* me sexually. She probably does not need sex so much, but I need her to want and need sex with *me*."

Earlier we described as a crisis the thinking that "men want more sex." Well, that's missing the point—which is that we need to take those words out of our vocabulary. To transform our thinking on this point, let's look at one of the greatest love stories ever.

Read Song of Songs 7:10 and write it on the lines below.

I belong to my love, and his desire is for me.
Song of Songs 7:10

_____

_____

Now read the verse aloud. Put the emphasis on the last word, *me*. Read it aloud again. Now put the emphasis on the word *desire*. The next time you find yourself thinking, *Here we go. He needs sex*, say this verse to yourself.

Song of Songs was written by a man who appreciated women. Inspired by God, this author created a beautiful love poem between a man and a woman. I think we can safely assume that the words he recorded as coming from a woman's mouth are words he would like to hear as a man. In another example of words a husband may hope to hear from his wife, the wife in Song of Songs 5:16 (*The Message*) describes her man in detail:
> "His words are kisses, his kisses words,
>   Everything about him delights me,
> thrills me through and through!
> That's my lover, that's my man, dear Jerusalem sisters."

Your husband may not be nearly as good with words, but there you have it: Your husband needs and desires *you*. He wants to be loved by you. You can now replace the thinking *Men want more sex* with your new understanding: *My husband wants to be desired by me.*

If you are married, your Weekly Challenge is to look at the messages you are sending your husband. Think about the last week or so as you answer these questions.

Is your husband receiving the message of Song of Songs 5:16 from you?
❑ yes ❑ no

When was the last time you sent your husband the message that "everything about him delights" you?

_____

What can you do to relay the message to your husband that he "thrills you through and through"?

_____

Your husband's immediate need for sex may seem physical, but it is so much more. He desires you, and he wants to be desired by you.

Searchlight

Read Genesis 2:20-25 in your Bible and thank God for His marvelous creation of the total sexual relationship. Now, read Genesis 2:24 one more time. Ask the Lord to reveal to you anyone or anything that is standing in the way of your being "one flesh" with your husband. Thank the Lord that He created you to be just the right mate for your husband. Ask Him to examine your bond and to reveal any weak areas on which you can work.

Song of Songs or Song of Solomon?
Different Bible translations use different titles for this collection of romantic poetry, with HCSB® using "Song of Songs." According to the *Illustrated Bible Dictionary* (Holman), the Hebrew title "Solomon's Song of Songs" means that this is the best of songs and in some way concerns Solomon. While the title appears to name Solomon as author, the Hebrew phrase also can mean for or about Solomon.

Your sexual interest touches the deepest of emotional needs in your husband. In the written survey comments and research interviews with men, I noticed two parallel trends—the great benefits a fulfilling sex life creates in a man's inner life and, conversely, the wounds that are created when lovemaking is reluctant or lacking. Today let's look at the benefits. First, may I ask you a question?

How do you think your husband defines "fulfilling sex"? Write your answer here. We will look at your response later today.

_____

_____

Lightbulb

Fulfilling sex makes him feel loved and desired and full of confidence in all areas of his life.

If You Are Single

God limits sexual relations to marriage. Part of the reason is protection from the devastating emotional affects that premarital sex can bring.

According to Hebrews 13:4, what does God say should be honored as pure?

_____

Whom will God judge?

_____

Are you beginning to see how deeply a man's sexual feelings go? By the way, as a single woman, realize that married men who are not getting their needs met are sometimes on the prowl. Guard yourself.

Marriage must be respected by all, and the marriage bed kept undefiled, because God will judge immoral people and adulterers.
Hebrews 13:4

Benefit 1: Fulfilling Sex Makes Him Feel Loved, Desired

Don't be fooled by appearances. To our husbands, making love is a source of so much more than physical release.

Making love is the purest salve for loneliness. One man who was interviewed said, "I feel like I go out into the ring every day and fight the fight. It's very lonely. That's why, when the bell rings, I want my wife to be there for me." Many men—even those with close friendships—seem to live with a deep sense of loneliness that is quite foreign to us oh-so-relational women. The physical relationship in marriage satisfies that need for him much like a good heart-to-heart talk does for us. He no longer feels like he is all alone against the world.

The sexual relationship is an expression of love to him even if it does not involve soft music and sweet words. You may have noticed that men sometimes make advances at times that seem least connected to the sexual. One woman shared that her husband wanted to make love after a funeral for a close relative. For him, making love was a comfort, a way of being wrapped in her love.

Beyond the feeling of being loved by someone, one of the most important aspects of this element of a man's inner life is his sense of being desired. Interestingly, what surfaced consistently from the men's survey comments was that a *mutually* enjoyable sex life is most critical to his feeling both loved and desired. The emphasis here is mine; don't miss it: He needs you to enjoy sex, too!

> **What are three adjectives that might describe how the woman in Song of Songs 3:1-4 was feeling?**

> _____   _____   _____

Every man wants his wife to desperately, anxiously, hungrily seek him. Nothing stops her.

> **What did she do in verse 4?**

> _____

When she found him, that big bear hug gave him the message and then . . . well, the rest is private, if you please!

> **From what you have read and heard so far, how do you think your husband would define "fulfilling sex"?**

> _____

> **Is this definition different from the one you wrote at the beginning of today's study?** ❏ yes ❏ no

¹In my bed at night I sought the one I love; I sought him, but did not find him. ²I will arise now and go about the city, through the streets and the plazas. I will seek the one I love. I sought him, but did not find him. ³The guards who go about the city found me. "Have you seen the one I love?" [I asked them].

⁴I had passed them when I found the one I love. I held on to him and would not let him go until I brought him to my mother's house—to the chamber of the one who conceived me.
Song of Songs 3:1-4

Spotlight
OK, it's time for honest talk! As you put yourself in your husband's shoes, ask yourself, *When was the last time I responded in such a way that he knew without a doubt that he was the most desirable man on the planet and that I never wanted to let him go?* As women, we understand what it means to want to feel desired. Who would have thought that so much of men's inner selves was also wrapped up in whether they felt desired?

Benefit 2: Fulfilling Sex Gives Him Confidence
By now, most of us have seen those television commercials in which a man's colleagues and friends repeatedly stop him and ask what's "different" about him. New haircut? Been working out? Promotion? Nope, the man tells them all, with a little smile. One man I interviewed brought up those ads.

"Every man immediately understands what that commercial is saying—it's all about guys feeling good about themselves. The ad portrays a truth that all men intuitively recognize. They are more confident and alive when their sex life is working."

Spotlight
Think about a time in your marriage when the sex was great (you may be in your best season now). Evaluate your husband's disposition.

How would you describe your husband during this season? Check all that apply.
- ❏ Energetic
- ❏ A spring in his step
- ❏ The same as always
- ❏ Gloomy and forlorn
- ❏ Cheerful, to the point of being silly

Now think of a time when things weren't so great in the bedroom. What was he like then?

_____

A whopping 77 percent of the men surveyed in the *For Women Only* research agreed that having sex with an interested and motivated spouse as often as he wanted would give him a greater sense of well being and satisfaction with life. This comment was typical: "What happens in the bedroom really does affect how I feel the next day at the office." Another man wrote: "Sex is a release of day-to-day pressures ... and *seems to make everything else better*" (emphasis mine). So, girls, when our husbands "feel better," that sense of wellness permeates the very core of their beings.

> *A capable wife is her husband's crown, but a wife who causes shame is like rottenness in his bones.*
> Proverbs 12:4, HCSB

In this translation of Proverbs 12:4, who do you think sees a husband's crown?

_____

What does "rottenness in his bones" do?

_____

We could paraphrase the verse this way: When a wife is the kind of wife a man needs, he shines like a crowned king. When a wife causes her husband to feel belittled, it eats at him deep inside. When sex is good, the husband likely will be affected in such a way that everyone will know. He will be energized and on top of the world. If he feels rejected or undesired as a man, he can feel ashamed, as if his very insides are being eaten away.

> *A hearty wife invigorates her husband, but a frigid woman is cancer in the bones.*
> Proverbs 12:4, The Message

Spotlight
Now read Proverbs 12:4 in *The Message*. Now get inside your husband's heart and write your own paraphrase of Proverbs 12:4. Begin with "When I ..."

_____

_____

_____

As we touched on in the Impostor study, your desire is a bedrock form of support that gives him power to face the rest of his daily life with confidence and well being. Conversely, when he does not feel desired by you, it cuts him to the core. Tomorrow we will see how deep those wounds can go.

A Word of Caution

If it is true that fulfilling sex makes a man more confident, more alive, more loved—then what happens if the sex is not fulfilling?

According to 1 Corinthians 7:5, what did Paul instruct Christian couples in Corinth not to do?

_____

The Apostle Paul spoke plainly to married couples about what goes on in the bedroom. Marriage partners need to be satisfied!

What is the danger of denying sex to each other?

_____

Do not deprive each other except by mutual consent and for a time, so that you may devote yourselves to prayer. Then come together again so that Satan will not tempt you because of your lack of self-control.
1 Corinthians 7:5, NIV

The danger is if we are not willing to ensure that our husbands feel desired by us, they could have a much more difficult time resisting that temptation elsewhere. Remember what a core need this is! Many a man has been led astray by the flattery of someone who, without the pressures of the day-to-day grind that you face, makes him feel like the most desirable man on the planet. The lure of the prostitute in Proverbs 7:15,18 is that she is looking for him and is available all night long. It's a love feast, and he's the main course!

The lure of pornography is another danger. If you are like me, you have puzzled over this one; I mean, it is just a picture, isn't it? Men have explained it this way: "It is as though that beautiful desirable woman is looking through the camera directly at me and saying, 'I want you.'" In today's world, the temptation to get that intoxicating feeling is at his fingertips 24/7.

I hope you are blessed with a man who is dedicated to honoring the Lord and you. Keep in mind, however, that he is a man. The Apostle Paul warns that as human beings we have limits. We can be tempted. To deny your husband or to not give the effort to make sex a fulfilling experience can be dangerous for your marriage.

Searchlight

How are you doing? I have kept our focus very narrow today, on what he needs and on the benefits he gets. Were you surprised at the extreme emotional ramifications about sex (or the lack of it)? Do you see any need for change?

Say again Romans 12:2, what I consider our study verse. Are you making progress in the areas God is revealing to you? To change habits and attitudes takes time and effort, but it is worth it.

Our study today may have reminded you of other facts about the inner lives of men. Wives can be good or capable in several ways as we show respect, trust his decisions, and build him up. Take a few moments to jot down in the margin some things you have learned so far in our study together

Once we see how central a fulfilling sex life is to a man's emotional well being, we need to know what happens in his heart when he doesn't get what he needs. That mystical bond of "one flesh" means that our rejection tears at his very flesh. To say no to intimacy translates to saying no to him as a man, which wreaks havoc with his emotions.

Lightbulb

A lack of responsiveness means rejection to a man.

Therefore, God's chosen ones, holy and loved, put on heartfelt compassion, kindness, humility, gentleness, and patience.
Colossians 3:12

If You Are Single

Read Colossians 3:12. Pray for your future husband if that is what you want. Plan now how you will show him compassion, kindness, and humility.

Complete this thought:
When I give myself in marriage, my husband will need from me

_____

_____

It Really Does Matter

Imagine that it is Christmas. The presents are under the tree. There is a beautiful box with your name on it. You know it is probably just what you asked for. You can't wait. Every time you pass the tree, you want to caress it. You can feel the excitement rising. The moment arrives for opening gifts. You reach for that beautiful, inviting package. Your husband says, "Oh no, I don't want you to open that one. Not today. Maybe next week."

What is your immediate reaction? _____

Who does he think he is? After all, it is your present, isn't it? Is he trying to hurt you? As it turns out, there is more vulnerability in a man's sexual advances than we have understood. Plenty of emotions are tangled up with what appears to us as a physical need for sex.

In a sense, when a man sends the signal that he wants to have sex with his wife, he is pulling back the curtain to his heart. Then, he stands there waiting to see if you are going to throw a dart at it.

If you don't agree and toss out the classic "Not tonight, dear," he hears, "You're so undesirable that you can't compete with a pillow … and I really don't care about what matters deeply to you." If you agree to have sex with him but don't make an effort to be engaged with the man you love, he hears you say, "You're incapable of turning me on even when you try … and I really don't care about what matters deeply to you." Either way, that is probably a different message than you meant to send.

Although we might only be saying we don't want sex *at that point in time,* he hears the much more painful message that we don't want *sex with him.* As it turns out, guys seem to take a little rejection more personally than we might have imagined.

It's Very Personal

Yesterday, I touched on a passage in the Bible that speaks very plainly to married couples. How good God is to make some things so clear for us in His Word.

Read 1 Corinthians 7:1-5 in the margin. According to verse 3, the marriage partner's focus should be where? _____

According to verse 4, your body belongs to whom? _____

And his body belongs to whom? _____

The Bible is not saying that we belong to our husbands in the sense of personal property that can be used or abused. Notice that verse 4 speaks to both of you. He has just as much responsibility to meet your needs as you do to meet his. However, remember that the focus of our study is narrow—on his privilege to have access to all of you.

Just like that Christmas present I spoke of earlier, your husband wants you to belong to him. That is why he has left his mother and his father—so he could cleave to you in marital intimacy. You are the one who completes him. I almost hesitate to use the word, but isn't Scripture telling us that he has a *right* to enjoy you physically? That's a wonderful gift!

A friend told me that this Scripture blew her away once she began to realize that marriage meant her husband had a right to expect sex with her. It was not a concession she could choose to extend to him or not.

Think honestly for a moment about what goes through your mind when you reject your husband's advances. Do any of these responses sound familiar?
- ❏ I have a right to a good night's sleep.
- ❏ I am just plain tired and rest is what I need.
- ❏ I can't be expected to meet everyone's needs all the time.
- ❏ I need some time to myself.
- ❏ I am not interested.

The emphasis on "I", while not subtle, helps us to remember our focus. Aren't we often quick to want to exercise our rights? To think "Well, it is *my* body!" But is it?

You are memorizing 1 Corinthians 7:4 this week. Say or read it aloud (p. 85).

When you deny him the sexual response he is expecting, you deny him access to part of himself. When a part of himself is missing, the wounds can go very deep.

The Deep Wound of Rejection

A man feels incredible rejection when his wife doesn't want to have sex with him. Keeping in mind that what he wants most is for you to desire him, let's look at the rejection issue from his point of view. To do so calls for us to first look at our own patterns of response.

When you say no to your husband's advances, what are some of the reasons for your response?

_____

¹Now for the matters you wrote about: It is good for a man not to marry. ²But since there is so much immorality, each man should have his own wife, and each woman her own husband. ³The husband should fulfill his marital duty to his wife, and likewise the wife to her husband.

⁴The wife's body does not belong to her alone but also to her husband. In the same way, the husband's body does not belong to him alone but also to his wife. ⁵Do not deprive each other except by mutual consent and for a time, so that you may devote yourselves to prayer. Then come together again so that Satan will not tempt you because of your lack of self-control.

1 Corinthians 7:1-5, NIV

In *For Men Only* (the companion to the *For Women Only* trade book), Jeff and I seek to explain to men that a woman needs a transition time for enjoyable sex. That is probably not going to happen when she is dead tired or her mind is full of other responsibilities. This says *nothing* about whether he is desirable to her; yet, even if a part of him understands that it has been a long day for her, another part senses personal rejection.

Just as you want him to understand your need at this point, you have to be very sensitive to his deep sense of rejection.

Circle any of the following scenarios that might apply to you.

NOT TONIGHT, DEAR

Have you ever considered he might be interpreting your "Not tonight, sweetheart" in one of these ways? ❑ yes ❑ no ❑ I need to consider the possibility.

One man summed up what I heard over and over again: "No' is not no to sex—as she might feel. It is no to me as I am." It does not seem to matter how irrational the thought process may be for the man. He knows his wife loves him. He knows she has been faithfully his for 25 years. He knows she is tired. The negative response is still like a dagger to his heart.

The Deep Wound of Emotional Turmoil

Feeling that his wife does not desire him wreaks havoc on a man's emotional balance. He can't just turn off the physical and emotional importance of sex, which is why its lack can be compared to the emotional pain you would feel if your husband stopped talking to you.

Spotlight
If your sexual desire for your husband gives him a sense of well being and confidence, how do you think an ongoing perception that you don't desire him translates in his mind? Write your thoughts here.

_____

As I have opportunity to speak to groups of men about our findings, I try to explain that a string of rejections doesn't necessarily mean that their wives are rejecting them as *men*; it could just be a busy week! I can tell you they scoff at this suggestion. They warn that any woman who consistently refuses her husband is sending signals that can undermine the loving environment she wants most. Her man can be left with a nagging lack of confidence. He can withdraw. As one man predicted, "She is going to have one depressed man on her hands."

Consider the painful words of this truly deprived husband—words that other men have described as heartbreaking:

> "We have been married for a long time. I deeply regret and resent the lack of intimacy of nearly any kind for the duration of our marriage. I feel rejected, ineligible, insignificant, lonely, isolated, and abandoned as a result. Not having the interaction I anticipated prior to marriage is like a treasure lost and irretrievable. It causes deep resentment and hurt within me. This in turn fosters anger and feelings of alienation."

This is an extreme case, but I mention it to show the depth of emotion involved with a man's need for his wife to desire him sexually. I certainly pray that this is not a description of your love life. It is time to stop and take stock.

Have you been tracking the messages you have been sending your husband this week?
- ❏ Yes, I am doing the Weekly Challenge.
- ❏ No, I have not.

How many times has your husband tried to initiate sex in the past two or three weeks? _____

How many times did you follow through with an affirming response? _____

How many times have _you_ initiated sex? _____

What is the overriding message your husband might have received from the messages you have tracked so far?
- ❏ I'm a busy lady.
- ❏ My job (or home) is of utmost importance to me.
- ❏ I love you and desire you, and nothing will keep me from you.
- ❏ I am available to you if you want it, but I'm not particularly interested.
- ❏ I'll do my duty.

I truly hope that you are beginning to sense compassion for your husband. Congratulations if you are doing well in this area. If you are still struggling, don't give up. God is able to change even the most intractable situation.

Searchlight

Read Colossians 3:12 in your Bible. When it comes to the way you respond to your husband's sexual advances, how does this verse describe your attitude? Are you compassionate to his needs or more worried about your own? Do you respond with kindness or with irritation when you are overly tired? Do you display humility, or do you have complete say over your own body? Are you gentle in your refusals, making sure he knows it is not about him? Do you, in patience, rearrange your list of priorities to meet one of his deepest needs? As you conclude today, use the margin to write Colossians 3:12 as a prayer.

If you need help
By the way, ladies, I recognize that some of you might very much wish that you could respond more wholeheartedly to your husbands' sexual needs but feel stopped in your tracks for various personal reasons. I don't want to add any more frustration but encourage you to get the personal or professional help you need to move forward. The choice to pursue healing will be worth it, for you and your man.

Most of us are not being manipulative to withhold something we know is critical to our husband's sense of well being. We are just busy running all over the planet. After a long day at the office or with the kids, more than likely we just don't feel an overwhelming desire to fling ourselves at our husband. His request for sex becomes one more item on our already-full to-do list.

Now that you are beginning to comprehend the truth behind your husband's advances, I hope you are *wanting* to respond. You may find that you need to respond in a different way. Responding the way he needs may mean making some changes.

Lightbulb
A man needs his wife to give priority to responding to him.

If You Are Single
Read 1 John 3:18-24 in your Bible. Are you currently in a relationship? Except for sexual needs, are you willing to put his emotional needs above your own? Is your heart condemning you of any words or deeds? Pray that God will help you respond in appropriate ways to your man with respect, compassion, and tenderness.

Get Involved
What images pop to mind when you hear the word *duty?* We do our civic duty by being responsible citizens who vote and pay taxes. We fulfill our obligations to organizations by carrying out the duties of an office. We "do our duty" no matter what. We're not always happy about it, but we get it done! Sounds very proper and unromantic, doesn't it?

A husband should fulfill his marital duty to his wife, and likewise a wife to her husband.
1 Corinthians 7:3

Read 1 Corinthians 7:3 again. What is the marital duty Paul was talking about?

_____

God talks about sex as a duty between spouses—and it is—but a man is devastated if he feels that sex is *only* a duty to his wife. Remember, he wants to feel desired and desirable.

We think we are doing our men a favor, and that is sex. The result for him is the same, isn't it? Well, in this case, not really. If you do respond physically but just to "meet his needs" without getting personally engaged, you are not meeting the needs I have been talking about.

Understanding the new revelations that you have had, how would you describe a woman's marital duty to her husband?

_____

In our follow-up survey with churchgoers, one man was particularly blunt. "The woman needs to play an active role in the sex life. She needs to tell her mate what she needs, wants, and feels. Passive wife = boring life." Whew! I also discovered that many of the men surveyed would be delighted if the wife would just make the first move once in a while.

I can't tell you how often I heard the appeal for his wife to not only desire him, but also to *do something* about it. Watch your husband light up when you decide to bring all your attentions and passion for him to bed with you. God has given us the gift of intimacy. Enjoy it!

Make a Loving Relationship Your Priority

For many women, sex is just not the priority that it is for men. And there are some good reasons. One woman I will call Gail, in an article for *Today's Christian Woman*, put the matter this way: "I felt what I did all day was meet other people's needs. Whether it was caring for my children, working in ministry, or washing my husband's clothes, by the end of the day I wanted to be done need-meeting. I wanted my pillow and a magazine."[1]

What are some "good things" that keep you busy at home, at church, or in your community?

_____

_____

_____

List some of the "loving" things you do for your husband to show him how much you love him.

_____

_____

_____

The Apostle Paul had a timely word for people who were busy doing good things. In 1 Corinthians 13, he addressed Christians about being Christian. He listed some of the good things they were doing: sharing with others, witnessing, knowing and understanding the Scriptures. Many New Testament Christians were sacrificing, showing benevolence, and working hard for the cause of Christianity, even to the point of martyrdom for some believers. However, Paul also gave the Corinthian Christians a pointed warning.

According to 1 Corinthians 13:3, what did they gain if their actions were not motivated by love?

_____

And if I donate all my goods to feed the poor, and if I give my body to be burned, but do not have love, I gain nothing.
1 Corinthians 13:3

Paul spent the rest of this chapter explaining that if love is not expressed in such a way that it meets the needs of others, it is like sounding brass and clanging cymbals, with absolutely no meaning. What a shame if all the love you feel in your heart and try to show with your actions doesn't really touch your husband's deepest needs.

Our friend "Gail," tired of "need-meeting," had an encounter with God. God prompted her to answer this question: *Are the "needs" you meet for your husband the needs he wants met?*

Write some things you do that tire you, drain your free time, cause you stress, or rob you of the energy you could devote to your husband?

_____   _____

_____   _____

_____   _____

When he has a desperate need to feel desired by you, how do you think he is interpreting the expressions of love that you are so busy offering day-by-day? Is the message getting through in the way you intended?

"Gail" reevaluated her priorities. Her husband did not seem to be as worried as she was about the laundry and the girls being perfectly attired. She began to realize that perhaps the world would go on if she didn't get the tires rotated right on schedule. While she was busy with lots of "good" things, she soon realized that she regularly said no to the one thing her husband asked of her. "Gail" lamented, "I'd been so focused on what I wanted to get done and what my children needed, I'd cut my hubby out of the picture."

Have you ever had an itch between your shoulders? You ask someone to scratch that hard-to-reach place. Up, down, no to the left. If they don't scratch the right spot, you are still left with an itch … and frustration on top of it. Similarly, are the many things that take your time and energy truly as important as this one? If one of his most vital inner needs is to feel desired by you and to experience responsiveness from you, can you afford *not* to spend the time and energy physical intimacy may require?

Plan a Strategy for Change

Now is a good time to reevaluate priorities with the help of your husband. Take the time to let him know that you are taking seriously his need for regular, satisfying sex. Do everything in your power to keep those pangs of personal rejection from striking the man you love.

Here is an example of how you might explain your new insights to your husband. On the lines that follow, write what you would say to your husband.
My words:
I have become aware of how important our sex life is to you. It is important to me, too. I am sorry if I have sometimes seemed to reject you. I could never reject you, for you are irresistible to me. Sometimes, I am just so overwhelmed and too tired to respond in the way I want to so badly. I now realize that your needs are different from mine. I want to be there for you. My body is yours. Help me to learn to be available to you.
Your words:

_____

_____

_____

The ways in which we respond to our husbands often become habit. Think about how you are accustomed to responding. Modifying habits may take time and energy, so plan a strategy for continuing change.

List changes you are willing to make in the way you do or say things. Feel free to check any of these that express good personal goals.
- ❏ I won't shrug and grunt a negative response. Instead, I will put my arms around him and explain that I would love to, but I need _____.
- ❏ I will agree to let the dishes go once in a while.
- ❏ I will agree to set the alarm 15 minutes earlier at least once a week.
- ❏ Before I automatically refuse, I will remind myself that I belong to him, and he belongs to me.
- ❏ I won't respond silently. I will look into his eyes and at least say, "I love you."
- ❏ Other: _____

_____

_____

Now that you know what you are willing to change, explain to him the help you may need in getting things done in such a way that you have more time or energy for him. I can't help but believe that if you explain to your man that you want to be more responsive but that you need help in eliminating some of the stressors, he will jump at the chance to say, "What can I do? Just tell me!"

Check some things your husband could do to relieve some of the stress that may hinder your responsiveness to him.
- ❏ Put the children to bed on nights we plan to spend time together.
- ❏ Be responsible for supper at least once a week.
- ❏ Agree to go to bed at the same time.
- ❏ Other: _____

Choose a relaxed time when you can talk in privacy. Speak to him with your heart. Leave him in no doubt that you love to love him.

Searchlight

God's Word tells us that we should consider our bodies as belonging to our husbands, and we should yield to them in love, respect, compassion, and tenderness.

Read I John 3:18-24 in your own Bible. You say you love your husband. Are you willing to put his needs above your own? As you have read today, or even this week, has your heart condemned you in any way? Have you made a promise to yourself and to God to do better? Remaining in Him gives us the promise of His presence and strength.

I know it may be difficult to change your mind about things you do not understand, but God is able to do in us what we cannot do on our own. Prayerfully keep that in mind as we continue our journey together.

Having heard so strongly in our research about the importance of sex to men, I urge you: This is one area in which you must not be slack in being the partner God intended you to be. Don't discount your husband's tremendous emotional need to be desired and loved by you. It is more important to him—and to your relationship and, therefore, your own joy in marriage— than you can imagine.

Lightbulb

A man needs his wife to be alert to his signals and sensitive to his needs.

If You Are Single

Offer Zephaniah 3:17 as a prayer for your future husband should the Lord lead you to marry:

> *"The LORD your God is among you, a warrior who saves.*
> *He will rejoice over you with gladness.*
> *He will bring [you] quietness with His love.*
> *He will delight in you with shouts of joy."*

Learning more about a man's inner life is preparing you to be a great life partner!

It Is Not Only for Him

As we discussed in the beginning of this study, our differences have been there from the beginning. In the classic book *Love Life for Every Married Couple,* Dr. Ed Wheat helps us celebrate the reason behind those differences between male and female. "In a loving, amazing, creative act, the almighty God conceived the wonderful mysteries of male and female, masculinity and femininity, to bring joy into our lives. … The person who refuses to see and rejoice in the fundamental differences between male and female will never taste the divine goodness God planned for marriage."[2]

"Divine goodness"—isn't that a fascinating way to think of your sexual relationship with your husband? Remember that woman was not created just to satisfy the physical need of man. When God created Eve for Adam, she was suitable for him in every way. God's plan for completeness included both of them. God laid the perfect plan.

Dr. Wheat continues, "Marriage always begins with a need that has been there from the dawn of time, a need for companionship and completion that God understands." Each partner gets those needs met in slightly different ways. This week I have tried to share with you the depth of your husband's need to feel desired by you. It profoundly affects his sense of well being and confidence in all areas of his life.

As you meet your husband's core need to feel desired and loved by you, he will reach out to meet your needs. I have heard hundreds of personal stories from women who validate this reality. Their husbands are so much more loving when they feel desired by their wives. Really, if he feels undesirable he will be on edge, grumpy, depressed. Conversely, if he feels desired, he's a sweet, loving man. You choose!

Getting the Signals Right, or Romance Redefined

In order to do all we can to support our man at this point, we need to get the signals right. We often misinterpret his signals because we think he is interested only in the physical. Are you getting the picture that while he is interested in the physical, sex is also very important to him emotionally?

Has your husband been sending you signals that he is unhappy about your responsiveness to him? It's possible that he may wish he could explain this to you, but doesn't know how. Maybe he has tried, but you have discounted the importance of his request. Maybe you just have not understood.

One of the most fascinating discoveries from my research has to do with how men look at romance. They really do want romance! We'll talk more about this later, but for now let me tell you how I began to realize that men define romance differently than we girls do.

Men find it romantic to do things together.

Playing together is very romantic for men. Having fun with their wives makes them feel close and loving and intimate; it offers an escape from the ordinary and a time to focus on each other—all things that women also want from romance. This means that going with him on an errand to the local hardware store may be terribly romantic for him!

One married man explained it this way, "For a guy, a big part of the thrill was doing fun things together. The woman who is having fun with her husband is incredibly attractive. If you see a woman out playing golf with her husband, I guarantee that all the other guys are jealous. Getting out and having fun together falls off in marriage because of various responsibilities, but men still want to *play* with their wives."

My eyes have been opened to all the times Jeff had suggested some activity that I didn't fully realize was romantic for him. In his mind, the activity wasn't just a fun day of hiking or a chance to relax and walk around a quaint little town—it was his version of a candlelight dinner. This recognition makes it much more fun to jump on the next opportunity, appreciating all that it means.

Spotlight

Does your husband ever invite you to come along to do something so off the wall that you have wondered, *Whatever is he thinking*?

Write some of those memories here.

_____

_____

_____

_____

What are some things your husband likes to do or places he likes to go outside the home? For which ones do you think he might like your company?

Write a few of those possibilities here.

_____

_____

_____

Romance without sex may feel incomplete for a man.

As the research consistently revealed, a guy wants romance to reignite the spark of dating, to reconnect after days of draining work at the office, to feel love and intimacy, to know he is wanted and enjoyed, and to utterly escape the crushing nonstop pressure of life. Sex can be a wonderful part of all that.

Sex doesn't always have to be connected to romance, and it doesn't have to happen at the same time—but trust me, it is in the back of his mind. To make a giant generalization, women can often experience emotional closeness and feel that an evening is romantically complete without sex—while men often cannot.

Many men expressed frustration and even heartache over times when they tried to be romantic, tried to do things that signal their love and care for their wives—and still didn't see any increase in sexual interest. Clearly, just as we want our husbands to love us in the way we need to be loved, so do our men want the same for themselves. Sex is a huge part of making them feel loved.

Spotlight

Has your husband ever set up a romantic evening that you ended with an "Oh, not tonight, dear"?

How do you think he feels when he is looking forward to a specific conclusion to an evening and gets rejected?

_____

One man put it this way, "I love setting up a romantic evening, but it is a lot of work for me. I don't think my wife realizes that when I am being romantic, I've got a very specific endpoint in mind. So, sometimes there's intense disappointment after all that work!" If you are missing your husband's signals, then it is safe to say that you are missing out on some romantic moments and some great sex!

When You Have to Say No

The truth is there are times when sex is just not going to happen. Men have told me that if a woman takes the time to explain her "no" then it can help. You cannot assume that he sees your briefcase full of reports or the pile of dirty dishes in the sink and automatically understands what is foremost on your mind.

Gently let him know what is going on inside of you at the moment. Leave him without a doubt that you desire him but that you are just not able to respond at the moment.

Leave him with hope! Make plans for a time when you can be fully devoted to each other. No other appointment should be as important as this one. Get a baby-sitter! Go away! Lock the door! Let your husband know he is irresistible to you.

Talk About It

Let's look at how an average couple, Anne and Mark, handled this important issue.

> Anne and Mark had been married for 15 years. Mark's business required him to work long hours. In the early years, Anne sat down with Mark and explained to him that she understood the long hours but what really hurt her was that he did not come home when he said he would. She told him that he was a great husband, but that this one thing made her feel very uncared-for. She told him that his willingness to tell her a realistic time when he'd be home and stick to it was—for her—one of the most important signals of his love. Mark understood and keeping this commitment became a priority for him.
>
> Now, years later, Mark noticed that their sex life had started to wane. Anne was not responding the way she used to, and seemed disinterested, busy, or tired. Physical intimacy seemed less of a priority to her than it had once been. Mark sat down with Anne.

If you were Mark, what would you have said to Anne?

_____

_____

_____

As they were talking, Anne realized she had not thought of the parallel between his need for sex and her need for him to be home when he promised. She began to understand that while she might be a "great wife" in every other way, if she didn't respond to her husband's sexual desires—one of his most important "love signals"—she was failing at making him feel loved. Mark said, "It clicked for her, and that changed everything."

Spotlight

Maybe your husband is not as open as Mark was, but has he given you hints by the comments he has made?

What have you have learned in this study that is changing how you view your husband's approaches?

_____

_____

_____

When the opportunity arises, talk with your husband about this important subject. If you need help getting to the heart of the matter, consider the following conversation starters:

- If I am simply too tired or preoccupied to be intimate with you, does this make you feel that I am rejecting you? If so, how can I communicate my inability at the moment without sending you a rejection message?
- Are there things I am doing for you that are tiring me but that are not a high priority for you? If so, can you help me understand your priorities? Can we develop a plan to accomplish what needs to be done so that we have more time for intimacy?
- How do you need to be loved by me? How can I best show you my commitment to you?

Searchlight

I want to close today by reminding you that God created woman as the man's helpmate. Rather than remaining overwhelmed by the responsibility God has given you, draw on the support He gives.

God is our refuge and strength, a helper who is always found in times of trouble.
Psalm 46:1

Read Psalm 46:1 in the margin. Who is the "helper" here?

_____

The Hebrew word used here to describe Father God is the same word used to describe the woman in Genesis 2:18. Genesis 1:27 tells us that man and woman were created in God's image. Could this possibly mean that we as women are created as helpers to our men in the same way God is always there for us—in good and in troubled times?

The LORD your God is among you, a warrior who saves. He will rejoice over you with gladness. He will bring [you] quietness with His love. He will delight in you with shouts of joy.
Zephaniah 3:17

How does God feel about having to meet our needs all the time? Find the answer in Zephaniah 3:17 and write it in your own words.

_____

Trust that God knows what He is doing. He delights in helping His children. As you obey Him, you will also find delight and joy. As you affirm your husband sexually, as you watch him blossom with your respect, and as you see him secure in your trust and admiration, you will feel delight.

Turn Zephaniah 3:17 into your prayer to the Lord. I've given you a way to start.
Thank You, Lord, that You take delight in helping me as Your child.
Lord, help me to …

As I respond to my husband, Lord, help me to …

Sex Changes Everything

For a man, sex fills a huge _____ _____ that cannot be met any other way.

That emotional need is to feel that his wife _____ him and _____ him.

If his wife responds out of _____, he feels _____ .

> ¹⁰*My love is fit and strong, notable among ten thousand.*
> ¹¹*His head is purest gold. His hair is wavy and black as a raven.*
> ¹²*His eyes are like doves beside streams of water,*
> *washed in milk and set like jewels.*
> ¹³*His cheeks are like beds of spice, towers of perfume.*
> *His lips are lilies, dripping with flowing myrrh.*
> ¹⁴*His arms are rods of gold set with topaz.*
> *His body is an ivory panel covered with sapphires.*
> ¹⁵*His legs are alabaster pillars set on pedestals of pure gold.*
> *His presence is like Lebanon, as majestic as the cedars.*
> ¹⁶*His mouth is sweetness. He is absolutely* _____ .
> *This is my love, and this is my friend, young women of Jerusalem.*
> Song of Songs 5:10-16

Machmad, the Hebrew root of the word *desirable*, means "the _____ of desire." It refers to whatever is precious to you.

Our husbands want _____ to _____ them.
The lure of pornography is not just the image but the _____ "I want YOU!"

So what's a woman to do?

Give the physical relationship _____ .

Making the first move occasionally is a _____ a wife gives her husband.

week five

Keeper of the Visual Rolodex

Ladies, this page should have a sign that reads "Sensitive Material Ahead." So let me ask you to stop right now and to pray—and then keep praying. Seek the Lord all week long, and ask Him to strengthen your heart as you continue being "transformed by the renewing of your mind." Now take a deep breath and promise to stay with me this week.

While most of us women realize that men are stimulated visually, did you know that it is an involuntary temptation against which they struggle *daily*? Some of us—especially the roughly 25 percent of women who indicate they are visually oriented—may have a sense for this. However, the majority of us haven't even known what "being visual" means, much less had any sense for what an overwhelming life factor it is for our men in this culture.

So what does a man's visual orientation mean? It means three things, as we will discover together this week:

1. Even the most godly, devoted husband cannot not notice a woman who has a great body and is dressed in a way that calls attention to it. According to my research results, a whopping 98 percent of the men said that if a woman with a great body enters a room, they are tempted to look at her—whether or not they actually do.

2. A related issue is this: A man carries in his mind a store of visual images of women, sort of like old snapshots or movie clips, and these images can pop up in his mind without warning, at any time. These images can recur even if he doesn't want them there. Then, once an image pops up, any man who wants to honor God or his wife in his thought life has to do the purposeful work to tear it back down.

Personally I struggled as I tried to come to terms with these findings. One day, in the car, Jeff and I were discussing what I was discovering and he confessed that he didn't understand why I was so surprised. The following exchange did more to teach Jeff and me how each of us is wired—and not wired—than almost anything else:

Jeff: "But you knew men are visual, right?"

Shaunti: "Well, yes, of course. But since most women aren't, I just didn't get it. I just don't experience things the same way you do."

Jeff: "See, I'm not sure I really believe that."

Shaunti: "Well, it's true!"

Jeff: "Maybe we just use different language to describe it. For example, think of a movie star that you find physically attractive. After we've seen one of his movies, how many times will that attractive image rise up in your mind the next day?"

Shaunti: "Never."

Jeff: "I must not be explaining myself correctly. I mean, how many times will a thought of what he looked like with his shirt off just sort of pop up in your head?"

Shaunti: "Never."

Jeff: "Never—as in never?"

Shaunti: "Zero times. It just doesn't happen."

Jeff: (After a long pause) "Wow."

3. And, finally, because men are so visual, it matters emotionally that a guy sees his wife being willing to make an effort to take care of herself for him. He doesn't want her to be a superhuman supermodel, but it does matter that she is willing to make the effort for him as well as for herself.

Ladies, I know from experience that some of this may be hard for you to hear at first, but stay with me and stay close to the Lord. I trust that the new understandings you will gain this week can help you be more supportive and protective of your husband in a culture that is very challenging for all of our visual men.

Lightbulb

Because men are visual, even happily married men struggle with being pulled toward live and recollected images of other women—and, at the same time, a man needs his wife to be willing to make the effort to take care of herself for him.

Weekly Challenge

As you go about your day this week, look for images that could be construed as "eye magnets" for a man. Make a mental note of what percentage of the women on television or in public might pose a constant challenge for a man who wants to honor his wife in his thought life. Evaluate your home environment for ways to help your husband in this effort.

Begin each day with a prayer that God will help you meet a new challenge. Practice every day. Continue to practice changes you are making from other Weekly Challenges.

As newlyweds, my husband and I lived in Manhattan, and like all New Yorkers we walked everywhere. I quickly noticed something strange. Quite often we would be strolling hand-in-hand, and Jeff would abruptly jerk his head up and away. We'd be watching in-line skaters in Central Park or waiting to cross the street in a crowd, and he would suddenly stare at the sky. I started to wonder, *Is something going on at the tops of these buildings?* It turns out something was going on, but it wasn't in the buildings.

Lightbulb

A man cannot *not* notice that attractive woman who is dressed in a way that calls attention to her figure.

To Not Look Is a Struggle

I asked a series of randomly selected Christian men who were serious about their faith and, if married, fully devoted to their wives, to respond to the following scenario.

> Doug, a successful businessman with a wife and kids, has traveled to California for a business deal. The conference room fills with top executives, so each one can give him a presentation. The first executive, a very attractive woman, walks to the whiteboard. She has a great figure, Doug notices, and her well-fitted suit shows it off tastefully. As she begins her presentation, the woman is friendly but all business.

Here is the question I posed: If you were Doug, what would be going through your mind as the female executive makes her presentation? Here are some of their answers:
- "Great body … Stop it! What am I thinking?"
- "I check to see if she's wearing a wedding ring."
- "I wonder if she finds me attractive."
- "It is hard for me to concentrate on her presentation because I'm trying so hard to look at her face and not her body."
- "I have to be ruthless about pushing back these images—and they keep intruding."

Ladies, I was amazed and dismayed; but after hearing similar reactions over and over from men I trusted, I realized this must be normal! Even if they fiercely strive and succeed in over-coming the temptation to actually *look*, men cannot *not* notice an attractive woman. The desire to look rises from deep within—and includes happily married, godly men. Proverbs 27:20 says, *"The eyes of man are never satisfied" (KJV)*.

A husband with a strong, happy 20-year marriage described a typical scenario:

> "My wife and I recently went out to dinner at a nice restaurant with some friends. The hostess was extremely attractive with a great figure and that spark that reaches out and grabs a man's attention. For the rest of the night, it was impossible not to be aware that she was across the restaurant, walking around.
>
> Our group had a great time with our lovely wives, but I guarantee you that our wives didn't know that every man at that table was acutely aware of that woman's presence and was doing his utmost not to look in that direction."

Spotlight

Have you noticed your man noticing other attractive women? What was your mental assessment of him at that moment?

While you may have had a few choice thoughts about what he was doing in these situations, you also may have experienced a sense of personal failure. As we delve more deeply into this subject this week, you will see how much of a core issue this visual nature is for him and how little it has to do with you personally.

I know from experience that right now as you are reading, some of you are getting quite upset, indignant, even angry. You may think I am excusing men for sinful, lustful behavior. Believe me, I'm not! Jesus was quite clear that a man who looks at a woman lustfully has already committed adultery in his heart! We must never wink and nod at sin, or say "boys will be boys."

In order to understand this extremely important subject—one that many men wish we could grasp—we need to look at it squarely and realistically. More importantly, we need to realize there is a critical distinction between temptation and sin. We'll talk more about this in Day 2; for the moment, remember, "Jesus understands every weakness of ours, because he was tempted in *every way that we are. But he did not sin!*" (Heb. 4:15, CEV, italics mine).

In order to jumpstart our understanding that this temptation is truly common to all of our men —even the good guys—let's visit again a fine man, Job.

How did God describe Job in Job 1:8?

_____

According to Job 31:1 what did Job promise not to do?

_____

Choose an answer for why Job had to make such a covenant.
- ❏ A "dirty old man," Job couldn't help ogling pretty women.
- ❏ Job struggled with a man's natural compulsion to look at attractive females and made a choice to honor God by not following his impulses.

God describes him as "the finest man in all the earth—a man of complete integrity" (Job 1:8, NLT). Surely, the "finest man in all the earth" wouldn't have this struggle! However, Job was a man like any other.

You love your husband as a man, and this characteristic is part of what makes him a man. Even if your husband is the finest man in all the earth, and even if you were a gorgeous model, your husband would still have this vulnerability. I know your first question is why did God make men to be so drawn to attractive women? I am not sure I can answer that except to say I am glad that my man was drawn to me!

Remember Adam's reaction to Eve in Genesis 2:23? Those who understand Hebrew better than I tell us that Adam was excited to see Eve. He was visually attracted to his new mate.

Then the LORD said to Satan, "Have you considered My servant Job? No one else on earth is like him, a man of perfect integrity, who fears God and turns away from evil."
Job 1:8

I have made a covenant with my eyes. How then could I look at a young woman?
Job 31:1

One of my closest friends relates that as a new bride at age 23, she was very shaken when she discovered that her sweet husband had this thought-life issue. She cried out to God, "Why did You create him like this?" Then she realized that God did create him like this, and He said His creation was good. We may be fallible, but we are created the way we are for a reason and a purpose. Be assured that God doesn't make mistakes.

Where were you when I established the earth? Tell [Me], if you have understanding.
Job 38:4

When Job asked God similar questions, God answered him with 129 verses but we can get the gist in one verse. According to Job 38:4, who is the final authority here?

_____

As we grapple with our whys, there is one thing we can be sure of: Sin corrupted God's perfect plan. Only God knows all His reasons, but we can presume that He designed men to be visual so that the *only* "great body" a man should get a good look at would be that of his wife! Men weren't supposed to be bombarded with the intensity of the temptations that they face every day in our sexualized culture!

We cannot understand all the intricacies of creation, but we can know that men seem to be created with two strong tendencies to be visually driven.
(1) A woman with a great body is an "eye magnet" who is incredibly difficult not to notice. Even if a man forces himself not to look, he is acutely aware of her presence.
(2) Even when no such eye magnet is present, each man has a "mental Rolodex" of stored images that can intrude into his thoughts without warning or can be called up at will.

A Mental Rolodex on Speed Dial

Remember how in the introduction to this week's study I mentioned that guys' brains store up visual images, images that can come back involuntarily? For those of us who aren't visual, it is hard to imagine that a man could have no control over something popping up in his head. But the survey demonstrated that this is indeed how men are built. Recognize that in our sex-saturated culture, the very act of living is a minefield of possible triggers and potential images that could be recalled days or even years later.

To use a common example, prime-time television commercials often flash sensual two-second images—say, of a woman undressing—that are up on the screen and gone before the man can look away. Nothing he can do. Boom, it's added to the mental Rolodex, whether he wants it to be there or not. It could pop back up in his head at any time in the future without warning—even if he doesn't want it there!

We know that the male population thinks about sex a lot. I did not realize, however, that this issue is not thinking about sex so much as picturing it. Fully 87 percent of men indicated that these images pop up in their heads.

You might be wondering, *What kinds of images?* Apparently just about anything: the memory of an intimate time with you (good) or the memory of a *Playboy* magazine (bad). It could be a recollection of the shapely woman who walked through the parking lot two minutes ago or an online site he saw two years ago. These images often arise without warning, even if the guy doesn't want them, or specific images can be recalled. As several men put it, "I have an unending supply of images in my head, stretching back to my teens."

When I asked how often a sensual thought or image barged into their consciousness, many men I interviewed said something like "all the time." Of course, I wanted to know what "all the time" meant! "If you're talking about a teenage boy, 'all the time' means *all the time*," one 40-year-old man explained. "It would be fairly unusual for a teenage guy to go a couple of hours without an involuntary image—and then when he does, he could spend half an hour straight on the subject.

"A 20-something man also has a pretty difficult time. Once you reach your thirties and forties, you're a little more settled and those thoughts are more often triggered by something." Once those thoughts are triggered, he and other men clarified, an image could rise up two or three times a minute! They also said that if the man is highly visually oriented, and if that temptation is entertained at all, it is even more difficult to get rid of.

Spotlight
If it is true that a man cannot *not* notice these visual stimulants, imagine what our culture is like for him. This week, notice the images that bombard men.

Think about the past 24 hours in your home. What opportunities has your man had to be confronted with sexual images?

The society in which we live is torture for men who want to honor God and their wives in this area. Temptation is everywhere.

So What Do I Do?
The first thing many of us need to do is make sure we are not adding to the temptation without even realizing it. Many current fashions seem to be designed to trigger a guy's visual temptation, and even women who want to be careful with their dress don't always know what does and does not pose a problem. Guys have told me that certain dress patterns can trigger this visual temptation. We'll talk more about this issue in Day 2, but if you want to look ahead, the sidebar "Ways to Champion Modesty" (pp. 118-19) pointedly addresses some of the issues he faces—and suggests possible solutions.

Second, beyond how we present ourselves in the world, we need to understand how this temptation affects the man closest to us and consider how to support him in his efforts to keep his thought life pure. For many of us, it would be so easy to move from understanding, to alarm, to the charge of the light brigade—to get anxious or suspicious and all fired up to change our men. Yes, men can and should do things to keep their thought lives pure. Yes, men can and should do things to honor the women they love. But this study is for women, for us alone. These revelations are meant to change *us*.

In today's world visual temptations are impossible to avoid. This compulsion in your man's life, whether or not he wants it to be there, is a constant burden for him.

According to Galatians 6:2, what should be our attitude toward the burdens that others face?

Carry one another's burdens; in this way you will fulfill the law of Christ.
Galatians 6:2

---

²Carry one another's burdens; in this way you will fulfill the law of Christ. ³For if anyone considers himself to be something when he is nothing, he is deceiving himself. ⁴But each person should examine his own work, and then he will have a reason for boasting in himself alone, and not in respect to someone else. ⁵For each person will have to carry his own load.
Galatians 6:2-5

The Apostle Paul recognized that everyone struggles. No one has the right to consider himself better than another because we are not carrying the same burdens.

Continue reading this Galatians passage. According to Galatians 6:4, what is the first step in being a support to someone else?

_____

As we consider any changes we need to make in our lives, we must first take stock of the condition of our hearts and our willingness to support our men in the way they need to be supported. Are you willing?

One man, from a follow-up survey of churchgoers, pleaded: "Encourage me rather than freak out and conclude the worst about me. The more I can reveal my weaknesses without being judged or accused, or without a major crisis in our relationship resulting from my transparency, the more I know I am loved for who I am, not for who she wants me to be."

Searchlight

Your memory verse for this week comes from I Corinthians 13. As you are called on to support your man as he needs to be supported, you will need the kind of love described in this passage.

Love is patient; love is kind. Love does not envy; is not boastful; is not conceited; does not act improperly; is not selfish; is not provoked; does not keep a record of wrongs; finds no joy in unrighteousness, but rejoices in the truth; bears all things, believes all things, hopes all things, endures all things.
1 Corinthians 13:4-7

Read I Corinthians 13:4-7 in the margin. Circle the characteristics of love that you feel you most need to face the visual element of a man's inner life. How would you describe this kind of love? Check all that apply.
❑ unselfish
❑ directed toward others
❑ goes against our natural inclinations
❑ sets aside my desires
❑ protects my rights

The Apostle Paul explained to the Christians at Corinth that as believers they should show the kind of love that goes against their natural instincts. Unselfish love comes from a relationship with God. You will need this kind of love to focus on your man's needs rather than on what you might want.

Do you have a personal relationship with God? If you do, then you have all the dimensions of God's love at your disposal. If you would like to know more about becoming a Christian, for yourself or your man, see page 173.

After months of financial stress, Blake and Nicole were grateful when Blake began a lucrative two-month filming job for a producer of athletic gear, even though it meant being out of town a lot. The video shoots were at a popular beach resort. On the phone one night Nicole joked to Blake that she wished she were "slaving away" in that environment too. Blake replied, "Actually, I wish you were here instead of me!" When Nicole asked what on earth he meant, he shut down and wouldn't explain.

Three weeks into the well-paying job, Nicole was surprised when Blake said he was going to turn the job over to a female colleague. When she asked him why, she was both surprised and dismayed when he confessed that he was having a "difficult time" being around women with great, athletic bodies in bikinis all day, and had begun being seriously tempted to turn on inappropriate movies in his hotel room at night. He was coming home.

Lightbulb
A man chooses what to do with the visual temptations he faces.

He Can Choose to "Take Every Thought Captive"
While you may be shocked at the graphic reality of this element of a man's inner life, the research revealed that this temptation is completely natural for 98 percent of men. It is so normal in fact, that the progression of response that we are dealing with is seen clearly in the lives of several men in the Bible.

Let's follow the story of one of them, David. Open your Bible to 2 Samuel 11. David was a man after God's own heart, a king of Israel. David's army was out to battle but David stayed behind in Jerusalem.

According to verse 2 what happened to David one night?

_____

Inner Step 1: For every man, sensual images and thoughts can arrive involuntarily and unexpectedly.
Man's initial temptation is often not only unintentional, but automatic. If the stimulus is there (a beautiful woman in a bathing suit), so is the response. As one man put it, "It doesn't even register that I thought *Great body* until two seconds later!" A man cannot prevent those *initial* thoughts or images from intruding. His brain reads *Great body* without his even realizing it.

David enjoyed the sight of her, so what did he do next? (See v. 3.)

_____

Inner Step 2: A man's involuntary physical impulse is to enjoy the feelings associated with these thoughts and images.
Because men are hardwired to be sexual hunters, every thought and image related to that pursuit comes associated with powerful feelings. When a sensual image enters a man's mind (or a great body enters his line of sight), it brings a rush of sexual pleasure—a short-term pleasure.

One married man told me when I interviewed him: "It is pleasurable—in a small way—in the same way that sex is pleasurable. Forcing myself to remove that thought from my mind is sometimes as difficult as it would be to stop in the middle of sex."

Remember the Rolodex of images and how they pop up? Another man wrote: "When an image plays on a man's brain or he gazes at an attractive woman, it's not just pure lust. There's a thrill there. A man can go back to that adrenaline rush by entertaining those images."

A New Testament writer calls this thrill "desire." What can desire do to a man, according to James 1:14?

_____

But each person is tempted when he is drawn away and enticed by his own evil desires.
James 1:14

In clinical research for my *The Lights of Tenth Street* novel, I heard over and over again how much men gravitate toward something that gives them an inner excitement, an illicit thrill—which helps us then understand why some men can get trapped by pornography.

Inner Step 3: Every man can make a choice—to dwell on the images and thoughts, to entertain the desire, or to dismiss them.
Hopefully, a man after God's own heart will deny himself this illicit desire in order to honor God, his wife, or his mental purity and thus establish deeper pleasure down the road.

He left all that he owned under Joseph's authority; he did not concern himself with anything except the food he ate. Now Joseph was well-built and handsome. After some time his master's wife looked longingly at Joseph and said, "Sleep with me." But he refused and said to his master's wife, "Look, my master does not concern himself with anything in his house, and he has put all that he owns under my authority. No one in this house is greater than I am. He has withheld nothing from me except you, because you are his wife. So how could I do such a great evil and sin against God?" Although she spoke to Joseph day after day, he refused to go to bed with her.
Genesis 39:6-10

King David chose not to follow that path. Second Samuel 11:4 tells us that David acted on his temptation and slept with Bathsheba. His temptation led him to sin because he acted upon his desire.

Let's look at another Old Testament example for a different outcome. According to Genesis 39:6-10, what golden opportunity faced Joseph?

_____

What was Joseph's reason for not doing as she wanted?

_____

Joseph took a stand because he knew that to follow this temptation would be a sin against God. Did his problem end there? Joseph had to deal with this temptation day after day. According to Genesis 39:10 he did everything he could to avoid Potiphar's wife.

Although few men can stop an involuntary image from popping up in their heads, and few men can stop themselves from *wanting* to look, like Joseph they can and do exercise the discipline to stop themselves from actually doing so.

Once an image intrudes in a man's head, he can either linger on it and possibly even start a mental parade, or he can tear it down immediately and take *"every thought captive to the obedience of Christ"* (2 Cor. 10:5). The temptation to look, the desire that flares up is not the sin. What a man chooses to do with that temptation can be a sin.

As we touched on in Day 1, this choice is the critical distinction between temptation and sin. Most of the men I talked to for my research take this choice extremely seriously. They make rigorous decisions to avoid unwanted visual invitations. They exercise the effort to turn away from those that do arise. When unwanted pictures arise anyway they use all sorts of diversionary tactics. Running through baseball scores and mentally checking off household projects were popular thought substitutes! Honestly, it sounds exhausting.

By the way, from the survey, the biggest factor in whether a man made this choice wasn't whether he was older, married, or happy in his relationship. It was whether he regularly attended religious services.

Spotlight

Have you noticed your man making an effort to avoid looking? Put yourself in his everyday world.

Does it require a lot of energy for him to avoid the "eye magnets" that come his way? What about his leisure activities—sports, movies, hobbies? Do they provide him with more or less opportunity to be tempted to visual stimulation?

It is vital that we understand just how much strength and discipline that choice requires so that we can appreciate what our men try to do for us every day in this minefield of a culture.

The Best Example

Think back to Nicole and Blake. Nicole was devastated that Blake would be tempted to look a second time at the women in bikinis or turn on inappropriate movies. She began wondering whether she could trust the man she had married.

In what ways was Blake honoring Nicole?

How might you have reacted?

You may be surprised and dismayed when you realize that your husband faces these visual temptations. But remember that Jesus understands and we can too.

Read Hebrews 4:15-16. If Jesus was fully man, what does this verse mean?

Jesus was fully human just as He was fully divine. Yet, is it hard for you to realize that He was "tested in every way as we are"? If men are wired to notice attractive females, then that means the pretty maiden caught Jesus' eye just as she would that of any other man.

For we do not have a high priest who is unable to sympathize with our weaknesses, but One who has been tested in every way as we are, yet without sin. Therefore let us approach the throne of grace with boldness, so that we may receive mercy and find grace to help us at the proper time.
Hebrews 4:15-16

Men make hard choices each and every day to honor their wives. Few may have to make the financial sacrifice that Blake made, but rest assured that many men make a valiant effort to avoid the sin here. But I should also acknowledge that some percentage of men will have grown really weary of that struggle, and some will have been making wrong choices. We cannot excuse it, but understanding it is the first step in having compassion and being willing to support their efforts to regain the purity of their thought lives.

Ways to Champion Modesty

Problem for him: Any outfit that emphasizes a woman's curves. Popular but tight Lycra®-type clothes that cling (and draw a guy's eye) to a particular body part will be problematic.

Solutions: Clothes that don't hug the body tightly are best. Either loosen or layer tops. If you can't bear to part with a favorite tight top, pair it with a cute jacket, vest, or cardigan.

With body-hugging skirts, pants, and shorts, there is no solution that will honor guys other than not to wear them or to pair them with a top that covers the tightest parts.

Problem for him: Outfits that allow "illicit" sight of skin (cleavage, more than a few inches of leg above the knee, or lower midriff or back).

You Can Champion Modesty in Yourself and Others

Let's face it, women who are totally clueless about this problem can thoughtlessly contribute to it. After all, the images in a man's mental Rolodex come from somewhere—and not just from pictures. The "eye magnets" on the street are choosing to dress the way they do.

Unfortunately, because many women are not visual, we may not understand what we are doing to the men around us—a fact that men often find hard to believe, by the way. When faced with his teenage daughter's choices in clothes, a friend lamented, "What is she thinking? Doesn't she know how the guy is picturing her?"

That is what we often don't get. Many women are just following the latest fashion trends. Others are longing for male love and attention, not realizing that the resulting attention is the wrong kind and has nothing to do with love. It's natural to enjoy being noticed, but he doesn't want you in his mental Rolodex.

You could be cluttering up a good husband's mind and tempting him to dishonor his wife by the way you dress. It is our responsibility to ensure that, as much as it depends on us, this does not happen.

So What Do I Do?

The most powerful and meaningful way to partner with our men is to pray for them. Psalm 127:1 tells us, *"Unless the Lord builds a house, its builders labor over it in vain. Unless the Lord watches over a city, the watchman stays alert in vain."* We can work to help and protect our husband and our marriage, but in the end, that's the Lord's job.

Open your Bible to Matthew 4 and consider Jesus' temptations. Before Jesus started His ministry, He spent 40 days in the desert praying. Satan came to Him there and tempted Him. The first temptation he threw His way was to use His power to meet a basic physical need, hunger. Jesus countered Satan this way: *"It is written: 'Man must not live on bread alone but on every word that comes from the mouth of God' "* (Matt. 4:4).

Pray that your man will lean on the Word of God when he is tempted to satisfy a physical desire. This works for you too. Lean on your memory verses as you work through these issues.

Next the Devil tempted Jesus with pride. He tempted Him to just see if God could handle the problem. Jesus answered him this way: *"It is also written: Do not test the Lord your God"* (Matt. 4:7).

Pray that your man will not push his limits. Pray for the courage to avoid visually stimulating situations when possible. Pray that you will be able to meet his emotional needs so that he will not be tempted to prove himself a man in some other way.

It is especially important that a wife prays for her husband instead of becoming the police. Counselors have told me that it will be very destructive to the relationship if the wife takes on the responsibility to police her husband.

Third, Satan tempted Jesus with power. He could have it all! This time *"Jesus told him, 'Go away, Satan! For it is written: Worship the Lord your God, and serve only Him'"* (Matt. 4:10).

Pray that your man will honor the Lord in everything he sees and does and that he will win the battle between temptation and sin. Pray the same for yourself.

Your husband needs your steadfast prayers more than anything else. As we do business with the Lord, we will also better understand what He wants from us. Our husband may need to do some work to bring his thought life back into purity. If so, as we pray, the Lord will be the One bringing to mind what he needs to keep his thought life pure— an accountability group, counseling, a male friend to whom he can talk and confess his failures, or even the realization (which for some men will happen for the first time) that this issue really is something that he needs to address.

Searchlight

Visual temptations are common to almost all men. Now you know that with the visual Rolodex that men carry around with them temptations to lust can be constant. Remember that the temptation is not the sin. Temptations come with being human.

What assurance does 1 Corinthians 10:13 give you?
"No temptation has overtaken you except what is common to humanity. God is faithful and He will not allow you to be tempted beyond what you are able, but with the temptation He will also provide a way of escape, so that you are able to bear it."

_____

_____

Thank the Lord that He understands what we all face. Thank Him that He can provide your man a way to escape his temptations.

Solution: Eliminate or cover up anything that doesn't pass this "mirror check." Using a full-length mirror to evaluate your outfits, look at what happens to your tops when you bend forward and to your skirts when you sit down.

Evaluate whether low-riding jeans are too low in front or in back and what someone sees from the back when you are seated.

Problem for him: Any sight of a woman's under-garments. Even if he could see the same thing at the beach, the sight of something he's not supposed to see is distracting.

Solution: Tighten bra straps so they don't escape, and ensure that nothing shows sideways through button-down shirts. *Never* wear a sheer top that shows your bra.

Inspect yourself from all sides in the mirror, ensuring that panty lines don't show from the back.

Many men echoed this husband's sentiment: "You have to realize: If men could, most would shut off their temptation to look at other women in a second. We loathe this temptation as much as our wives do!" They may go through exhausting mental gymnastics often each day as they deal with the inner element of being visual. Half of the men responding to our follow-up survey of churchgoers said they try to stop themselves from looking. Is there anything we can do to help them?

Lightbulb

A man's struggle with the temptation to "look" has very little to do with you.

Just Imagine

Unless you are one of those women who experiences visual temptation, you are probably having a hard time grasping the full impact of this revelation about the inner lives of men. But, if it is true, then what does it mean for your man?

Once I asked an audience to think about the Weekly Challenge question you are considering: What is our culture like for men who struggle with these visual temptations? From the crowd, a lone man's voice rang out, "Hell."

In this word search, circle visual minefields a man has to face each day.
(Key on page 123.)

T	E	L	E	M	I	S	C	E	P	T	O	R	I	A	L	E	D	A	P	T	O
M	O	N	E	C	T	I	P	A	N	O	M	A	G	A	Z	I	N	E	S	E	T
P	A	S	P	O	R	T	I	N	G	E	V	E	N	T	S	E	N	T	E	A	S
E	N	R	I	N	M	E	N	T	O	E	B	I	L	L	B	O	A	R	D	S	A
M	A	D	V	E	R	T	I	S	E	M	E	N	T	S	R	A	M	O	E	D	S
N	O	A	D	R	O	N	T	V	P	R	O	G	R	A	M	S	E	R	T	M	O
A	M	G	O	C	O	M	M	E	R	C	I	A	L	S	A	T	D	R	E	C	K

Not all triggers are visual. Radio talk shows, comedy routines, music, jokes, magazine articles, and tabloids at the grocery store checkout can trigger sexual images just as frequently and vividly. Imagine a man having to make a conscious effort to avoid each stimulus in a normal day. If he is successful in turning away from an "eye magnet," what about the effort to control the mental images that may pop up from his mental Rolodex? It is so natural for him to look and so hard for him to forget what he has seen.

Read these Scriptures and underline words or phrases that describe how keeping a pure thought life is a constant struggle.
Galatians 5:17
"For the flesh desires what is against the Spirit, and the Spirit desires what is against the flesh; these are opposed to each other, so that you don't do what you want."
Romans 13:13-14
"Let us walk with decency, as in the daylight: not in carousing and drunkenness; not in sexual impurity and promiscuity; not in quarreling and jealousy. But put on the Lord Jesus Christ, and make no plans to satisfy the fleshly desires."

When a man is dealing with temptation, it is good to have someone to whom he can be accountable. Marriage counselors tend to believe that, although there needs to be an open husband-wife dialogue, the husband's primary accountability partner should be male.

If your husband has a serious struggle with dangerous or addictive behaviors, specialized help and resources are required.

Mark 14:38
"Stay awake and pray so that you won't enter into temptation. The spirit is willing, but the flesh is weak."

Second Corinthians 10:3-4
"For although we are walking in the flesh, we do not wage war in a fleshly way, since the weapons of our warfare are not fleshly, but are powerful through God for the demolition of strongholds. We demolish arguments and every high-minded thing that is raised up against the knowledge of God, taking every thought captive to the obedience of Christ."

Spotlight

Imagine the mental energy that your man spends on this struggle in a normal day. It must be exhausting!

And Now for Some Reassurances

I have tried to give you an idea of what this visual element is like for men. Now I want to encourage you by looking at some reassurances of what it is not.

Reassurance #1: His temptation is often not primarily sexual.

One man I interviewed told me, "What you may not realize is that a lot of this is simply about admiring beauty. It is pleasurable to look at that good-looking woman. It's like looking at a painting or walking through an art gallery. A man may look, despite himself, but it's not necessarily a sexual thing."

Reassurance #2: Every man is different.

Every man experiences a different level of visual temptation. For some men, an involuntary sensual image may be little more than a nuisance. Others might find it a real stumbling block. Some men may be able to handle a sexy advertisement while others have a difficult time with it for days. Since everyone is different, we shouldn't jump to conclusions or pass blanket judgments.

Reassurance #3: It's not because of you.

Upon learning about this visual element, we secretly wonder if our husband's struggle arises because of our flaws. Here is the good news: It is not about you! One woman shared how relieved she was when she discovered that this response was built into her man. "For years," she said, "I thought it meant that I was less than he needed. I was too old or too fat. What I really felt in my heart was that he was being unfaithful to me just by having this temptation!"

Reassurance #4: This doesn't impact his feelings for you.

Most important (and perhaps hardest to get) is this fact: A man's human temptation has, as one man put it, "no impact whatsoever on my feelings for my wife."

According to Proverbs 5:20-23, what are the consequences of being caught up in sexual sins?

Why, my son, would you be infatuated with a forbidden woman or embrace the breast of a stranger? For a man's ways are before the Lord's eyes, and He considers all his paths. A wicked man's iniquities entrap him; he is entangled in the ropes of his own sin. He will die because there is no instruction, and be lost because of his great stupidity.
Proverbs 5:20-23

_____

_____

Many men spend a lot of energy to avoid being entangled in a trap that could cost them the loving relationship they have with their wives!

Spotlight

Has your husband ever tried to reassure you that he was not interested in someone just because he thought she was attractive? Did you believe him?

A man who has been married more than 25 years explained it this way:

"There is no relationship with the woman who catches your eye. With your wife, you have a deep and long and meaningful relationship. There is no competition there. Yes, your mind may make the observation that this other woman is 20 years younger and has never had two kids. But that is all it is—an observation. And that observation is immediately offset by other factors, such as the fact that you love your wife!"

So What Do I Do?

The key is to understand what is helpful in *your* marriage. Tell your husband that you understand the difficulties he must face every day and that you are willing to talk; as we've already mentioned, don't try to "police" him. Instead, ask what you can do to help. Put yourself on his team to help him win this fight.

Jim and Becky worked out a system to handle the visual temptations Jim faces as a businessman who travels and does business in exciting places. At a meeting Jim's attention was drawn to a very attractive woman across the table, who he knew he would have to meet with again.

After the meeting he called Becky and said, "I had a real visual struggle with this woman in my meeting. Will you pray?" It was never easy for Becky to hear these confessions but their plan worked, so she started to pray that if Jim saw the woman again she would even repulse him.

The next time Jim had a meeting at this business, Becky's phone rang. "I don't know what I ever saw in her," Jim wondered. Becky thanked God for His answers to her prayers.

What effort was needed on Becky's part?

_____

_____

How do you think being free to call his wife affected Jim?

_____

_____

Becky understands that the temptation to dwell on some attractive "eye magnet" is part of being a man for Jim. Yet, she struggles with hurt feelings when she hears his confessions. "When he tells me about the cute girl at the office, I go crazy. I start planning to lose 10 pounds immediately, but the Holy Spirit prompts me to pray (for herself and for him) instead of letting my thoughts run wild." Becky follows through with their plan because of the support it provides her man and the ultimate peace it brings to their relationship.

Notice and appreciate your husband's efforts to honor you. Now that my radar is on, not only does my husband not resent my new awareness; he actually appreciates it. Because now I see the girl with the great figure—and I notice when Jeff is tense with the effort of "not looking." Instead of being upset, I love him for the effort he is making to honor me.

Choose the option that would show the man that his wife appreciates his struggle and the efforts he is making.
Mandy noticed Brandon turning away from the Victoria's Secret commercial. She
❏ gave him one of her special grins, mouthing the words, "Thank you."
❏ tapped her foot loudly on the floor to make sure he knew she saw him looking.

A gentle word and an understanding spirit from you will help your man tremendously If he is a man who has had more bumps in the road in this area—if he does sometimes give in—that peaceful spirit can be powerfully used by the Lord to approach the issue with him in a spirit of concern rather than condemnation.

Searchlight
You cannot change the way your man is wired nor can you blame him for the existence of the temptation. You can make an effort to put yourself in his shoes and try to understand—even if, sometimes, you will not agree with his actions or thinking.

Over and over in this study you are being asked to take the high road and to let God work in your husband's heart. If you choose to put your man's feelings and needs before your own, you will likely experience a new peace in your heart—especially if one of those needs is special help in this difficult area.

Read Colossians 1:9-14. Using Paul's prayer for the Christians at Colosse as a model, write a prayer for yourself on a separate piece of paper. Seek God's help in understanding and doing what you need to do to encourage your man.

Answers to activity on page 120.

For this reason also, since the day we heard this, we haven't stopped praying for you. We are asking that you may be filled with the knowledge of His will in all wisdom and spiritual understanding, so that you may walk worthy of the Lord, fully pleasing [to Him], bearing fruit in every good work and growing in the knowledge of God.

May you be strengthened with all power, according to His glorious might, for all endurance and patience, with joy giving thanks to the Father, who has enabled you to share in the saints' inheritance in the light. He has rescued us from the domain of darkness and transferred us into the kingdom of the Son He loves, in whom we have redemption, the forgiveness of sins.
Colossians 1:9-14

```
T  E  L  E  M  I  S  C  E  P  T  O  R  I  A  L  E  D  A  P  T  O
M  O  N  E  C  T  I  P  A  N  O (M  A  G  A  Z  I  N  E  S) E  T
P  A (S  P  O  R  T  I  N  G  E  V  E  N  T  S) E  N  T  E  A  S)
E  N  R  I  N  M  E  N  T  O  E (B  I  L  L  B  O  A  R  D  S) A
M (A  D  V  E  R  T  I  S  E  M  E  N  T  S) R  A  M  O  E  D  S
N  O  A  D  R  O  N (T  V  P  R  O  G  R  A  M  S) E  R  T  M  O
A  M  G  O (C  O  M  M  E  R  C  I  A  L  S) A  T  D  R  E  C  K
```

You have learned how attracted men are by the visual. Earlier this week, we discussed the importance of championing modesty in our dress, so as not to add to men's visual temptation in this culture. We emphasized that the existence of this temptation says nothing about how much a man loves his wife or girlfriend. However, there is one area in which a wife especially should think through what her husband's visual nature might mean for her, not out in the world but at home.

In Christian settings, it often has become off-limits to emphasize the importance of a woman's physical appeal; but I think we need to talk about it here because I heard so much about it, in confidence, from many caring husbands. We think that if God does not look on the outward appearance, then neither should our husbands, right? The truth is that because we know "It's what's inside that counts," we can easily migrate to the idea that what is outside doesn't matter. It does.

In the research survey, 70 percent of men indicated they would be emotionally bothered if their wives let themselves go and *didn't seem to want to make the effort to do something about it.* Only 12 percent said it didn't bother them.

So hold onto those hard hats, girls. What's on the outside does matter. When we seem to be willfully ignoring that truth, our men—even godly men who are devoted to us—end up feeling disregarded, disrespected, and hurt.

Lightbulb
The effort you put into your appearance is extremely high on your husband's priority list; yet, the chance is extremely low that you know his true feelings.

Out, Blind Spot
Call me naive, but I didn't realize that the issue of appearance was such a big deal. Knowing how visual men are, I should have had a clue. Somehow I assumed that if I was out of shape, I was the only person who was negatively affected! After speaking to a group of both men and women about other topics in this book, I was approached by a colleague whom I will call Ted. Looking rather uncomfortable, he shared the following:

> "I think women have a blind spot in an area that they really need to understand. I don't think women know how important it is to take care of themselves. … See, my wife is 115 pounds, but her weight isn't the issue. It's not about being tiny. If she doesn't take care of herself, dresses sloppily around me all the time, never exercises, and has no energy to go out and do things together, I feel like she's choosing not to do something that she should know is important to me. … But really, I just want to see that my wife cares enough about me to *make an effort."*

What is your reaction to his comments?

_____

Most of us can become paralyzed into inaction by the thought of having to look like the impossibly thin 20-year-olds on TV. Yet, over and over again, I heard men say that what mattered most was not that their wives shrank down to honeymoon size, but that they were willing to make the effort *to take care of themselves* for him.

The survey supported this response. Five out of six men agreed—with regular churchgoers agreeing even more strongly. Results do matter, but they will be a by-product of our efforts to take care of themselves.

Why Does Your Effort Matter?

One day I overheard my husband and my book agent, Calvin, talking in the other room. Jeff was telling Calvin about the time "Ted" first brought up this subject—and the surprise I felt at what I heard.

> *Jeff:* "I was stunned when she said she'd had this great conversation with this guy and started sharing all the surprising things he'd said. I was thinking, *What about that* didn't *you get before?!"*
> *Calvin:* "They know it's important, but not how essential it is."

So why is it so essential? Here's what men said when they felt safe enough to tell the truth.

1. "When you take care of yourself, I feel loved."

Because this area is so imperative to them, our efforts— or lack thereof—directly affect their perception of our care for them. Seeing us make the effort to look good makes them feel loved and cared for. It matters to them in the same way it matter to us when we notice our husbands making an effort to do things that make us feel loved—especially those things that are difficult or don't come naturally. If your husband truly puts effort and thought into a romantic event, do you really mind if it's not perfect? Of course not. You feel loved and cared for.

Consider one husband's honesty: "My wife is trying to slim down right now, and it makes me feel like a million bucks. I know she's also doing it for herself, but the fact that she cares about how she looks is a total turn-on, if you want to know the truth. I tell her all the time how much I appreciate the work she's putting into this."

Maybe you do exercise and watch what you eat. If not, what could you do to take better care of yourself?

_____

Have you ever noticed a positive response from your man in relation to your appearance or your efforts to take care of yourself? Whether he verbally affirms you or not, his inner response is to feel loved and cared for. He'll appreciate the effort you are making for him and for yourself.

Imagine your husband saying to you the words of Song of Songs 4:9. How does that make you want to respond?

_____

Understanding more of this visual element will (check all that apply)
- ❏ make me more attentive to my day-to-day appearance
- ❏ encourage me to exercise more
- ❏ affirm my efforts to make myself attractive when I am around my husband

[9]"You have captured my heart, my sister, my bride. You have captured my heart with one glance of your eyes, with one jewel of your necklace. [10]How delightful your love is, my sister, my bride. Your love is much better than wine, and the fragrance of your perfume than any balsam."
Song of Songs 4:9-10

Making the effort to take care of yourself to make him feel loved ends up making you feel more loved. How can you lose?

2. "When you don't take care of yourself, I feel unvalued and unhappy."
How does a man feel when the woman he is married to looks significantly different than the one he courted? After I tackled this subject in one of my newspaper columns, a 27-year-old man wrote to tell me he knew a number of men who love their spouses, but are not happy, mainly because their wives had gained a lot of weight since their wedding day.

He made this comparison: "Shaunti, those women need to realize that their doubling in size is like a man going from being a corporate raider to a minimum-wage slacker—and assuming it has no effect on his spouse."

> Michelle told us she had read *For Women Only* and had had her eyes opened about how visual men really were. She was also challenged to take off the extra weight she had put on over the past 10 years. She found a good, low-carb diet, started exercising, and soon 30 pounds came off! Although her husband had never said a negative word about her appearance, suddenly he lit up with excitement about her success—and encouraged her with renewed praise and affection. Oh, why hadn't she done this sooner?

If Michelle's husband was proud of his wife before, how do you think he must feel now?

_____

Is it wrong of him to feel this way? ❑ yes ❑ no

Remember how much a man likes to do things with his wife, how close that makes him feel to her? I frequently heard men say how sad they felt when their wives don't have the energy or desire to do things together. One survey respondent wrote, "She is a very pretty woman, but she is not taking care of herself so she feels bad about her looks and has little energy. We are limiting our opportunities such as going to a pool party, or the lake, or beach."

Does this subject make you cringe, anger you, or stir up another strong emotion? If so, why do you think that is the case?

_____

Does it help to know that "it's not about being a size 3" and that "it's all about the effort"? ❑ yes ❑ no

In a way, this issue for men is like romance for us. Maybe it shouldn't matter whether our husbands ever put one jot of effort into romancing us, but it does. We love him regardless; yet, we still feel that empty wistfulness for what could be.

Guys feel the same way about our appearance—or at least our effort. It is important that we acknowledge that this male desire is both real and legitimate.

So What Do I Do?

If you're pretty sure this topic was meant for you, but you want to run it by your husband first, my recommendation is simple and heartfelt: *Don't.* Think about it—if your husband approached you about this, no matter how gently, what would you do? Probably burst into tears as I have done in similar circumstances. That is enough to make most men so distressed and uncomfortable that they will never bring it up again. Most men are willing to preserve their wives' feelings at the expense of their happiness so they don't feel the freedom to deal with this issue openly and honestly.

Jeff suggests this rule-of-thumb: If you are not *realistically* happy with your *overall* appearance and fitness level, assume he is not either. Don't make him tell you—both for your sake and the sake of your future together. (For the sake of your sanity, note the words *realistically* and *overall*. We're not talking about someone who is fit and trim, but thinks she needs to lose five pounds or is dissatisfied with a certain feature. We are only talking about those things we can healthfully change, if we need to.)

A man gets very frustrated when the woman in his life endlessly anguishes about her appearance—but takes little or no meaningful action.

Has your man suggested—or perhaps even hinted—that your appearance is an issue with him?
❏ yes ❏ no
How did you respond? Did you see him making himself vulnerable to bring up something that is important to him?

_____

Are you "realistically" happy with your overall appearance and physical well being?
❏ yes ❏ no
Do you need to set some goals for yourself? If so, write them here.

_____

Many comments on the survey echoed this one: "If she wants to look better, she needs to do something about it, not just complain about it all the time."

Searchlight

Say aloud your Week 1 memory verse: *"Therefore, brothers, by the mercies of God, I urge you to present your bodies as a living sacrifice, holy and pleasing to God; this is your spiritual worship. Do not be conformed to this age but be transformed by the renewing of your mind, so that you may discern what is the good, pleasing, and perfect will of God"* (Rom. 12:1-2).

I hope you have been encouraged that men don't expect us to be models, but we have been reminded that we are accountable for our physical well-being and appearance. Who doesn't want the relationship benefits that come our way when we show our men we care enough about them to give our appearance a little effort?

Knowing that our men cannot help but be stimulated visually is hard to grasp. What most women really want is for their men to only have eyes for them. As we struggle with these hard truths, it might be helpful to remember that we are not the only ones struggling.

We're also asking our man to do something that is hard and goes against his natural instinct. The man who originally opened my eyes to this issue explained it this way: "We need to see that you care about keeping our attention on you—and off of other women. Sometimes it is so hard for us to look away. It takes a lot of work and effort. It helps me so much if I see that my wife is willing to do her part."

Lightbulb
A man wants to see that his wife cares enough about him to make an effort.

The Plain Truth

In the Book of Esther, Queen Vashti greatly disrespected the king by not appearing at his summons. Why did he call her to come to the feast? According to Esther 1:11, He wanted "to show off her beauty to the people and the officials, because she was very beautiful."

A man's wife is an extension of himself, just as he is an extension of his wife. Most men know that the appearance of their wives complements them in the presence of other men. I offer as proof these comments of a close friend whose heart I trust completely:

> "Sometimes I'll meet a guy who looks just like an average guy. But then, if I meet his wife and she is huge and very out of shape and just sloppy, I feel so sorry for him. It sounds terrible, but my gut just churns for him. It's this 'Oh, I'm so sorry' sort of compassion. That sounds absolutely terrible to say, but it is what every man is thinking.

> "But then sometimes I'll meet a man whose wife is overweight—but she takes care of herself. She puts some effort into her appearance. She dresses neatly, or does her makeup and hair. If she is comfortable in her own skin and is confident, you don't notice the extra pounds. I look at that husband and think, *He did well.* "

I was so confused by this seeming contradiction that I asked Jeff to help me sort it out. Is it looks that matter or confidence? "There's no getting around the fact that men are attracted to looks," he said, "but looks are just one part of the package, and it is the whole package that is important."

Since I was still struggling to understand, Jeff thought for a minute and then mentioned the names of two married women we both know. One is a very slender, willowy blonde with a perky personality. The other is middle-aged, no longer slender, with a gentle, confident air, and a sharp mind. Jeff explained, "They look entirely different, but both are attractive—physically attractive even. I think both their husbands did very well."

How does Jeff's explanation make you feel? How comfortable are you in your own skin?

Have you ever ever perceived that your appearance was important to your husband when you were with others?
❏ yes ❏ no
How did that make you feel?
❏ irritated ❏ flattered ❏ confused ❏ didn't affect me
How might you interpret that importance now?

_____

The way you dress and carry yourself speaks volumes about both you and your husband. You may not like the idea that others are judging your husband on your appearance, but according to the men I spoke with, it happens often. Making judgments based on appearance comes naturally for men because visual attraction is such a core issue.

Good News in Abundance

At this point, some of you may be throwing up your hands. If effort is really what matters, how, you wonder, are you supposed to add this effort to many others? Once you decide to take action, some good news opens up to you. As it turns out, the person who cares so deeply about your appearance is, in almost every case, ready to be part of the solution.

Good news part 1: Your man wants to help you.

Almost every man I surveyed said he would do whatever it takes to help his partner make this particular effort. Actually, only 4 out of 400 said they would be unwilling to help. One guy told me, "If a guy's wife suddenly verbalizes that she's determined to drop some weight and needs his help, any guy is going to jump to it! 'What can I do? Here's a credit card!'"

My husband drew a youthful comparison. "Look," Jeff said, "when we were teenagers, the guys were always busy playing football or whatever. But if our girlfriends needed a ride to the tanning salon, we'd drop everything and drive them in a heartbeat. We'd even give them money to go! It was in our best interest! And that feeling doesn't change as we get older—we're willing to help our wives. What changes is the busyness of our schedules. But even then, there are things almost any guy can and will do to help if he sees that you are serious about it."

Check some things your man could do to help you make the effort to take care of yourself. He could:
❏ watch the kids in the evening so you can walk
❏ drive the soccer carpool so you can work out
❏ stop bringing home certain kinds of food
❏ cook dinner so you're not tempted
❏ diet with you

What could you ask him to do?

_____

Be willing to ask him to help—and then take him up on it! Remember, since it's your sincere concern and effort that matters most, you can expect to see relationship benefits coming your way very soon.

Good news part 2: The revolution in the resources can help you.
Thankfully, there has been a revolution in our scientific understanding of what eating well actually means (good carbs and good fats versus bad ones). If you're like me, knowledge is the key to making a complete lifestyle change. Several well-respected books are now available on what it really means to eat well and thus maintain a lifelong healthy weight. (On a personal note, I feel like I can stick with my new eating habits for the rest of my life because of the education I gained from *The South Beach Diet* by cardiologist Dr. Arthur Agatston.)

Good news part 3: God will help you.
You probably feel battered by all of this information, so let me encourage you: God will help you address this health and fitness issue in amazing ways, once you realize the need.

Look up these verses, and match each passage to a central truth.
___ 1 Corinthians 6:19-20   ___ a. don't let your stomach be your god
___ Romans 6:11-13   ___ b. control your desires
___ Philippians 3:19   ___ c. glorify God in your body

Now that my eyes have been opened to the fact that my efforts are actually so important to my husband (and, conversely, that my lack of effort is so hurtful), you wouldn't believe the difference it has made in my motivation. I feel like the Lord has blessed my desire to serve my husband and our marriage by giving me a permanent internal motivation to have a healthy "temple." I know He will do the same for you.

Changing Your Pattern
You now know that your effort to take care of yourself is important to your husband. Plus, as we discussed in Day 2, our effort to be modest in our appearance is important to the mental Rolodex of someone else's husband.

Picture this: A man goes into the worship center and takes a seat. A few rows ahead, he notices a young shapely woman taking her seat—wearing a tank top! We don't want men to add images of us to their mental Rolodexes, but that is exactly happens. Our understanding of his visual nature should have huge ramifications for how we, and our daughters, choose to dress. First Timothy 2:9 encourages women to dress modestly, especially in a place of worship.

How is your thinking affected by how deeply men are impacted by a woman's appearance?
❑ I need to rethink my business wardrobe.
❑ I realize I have used my clothes to call attention to myself.
❑ I need to take more care with my appearance.
❑ That's their problem, not mine.
❑ I need to dress my best for my man's eyes.
❑ I need to talk to my (daughter/niece/cousin/friend) about her wardrobe.

When I was growing up I assumed that the rule of modesty was just a way to keep me from having fun! I thought modesty was for my sake. Now, I realize that the biblical command to modesty is also for the man's sake.

Fighting the Temptation of Today's Culture

As we end our study about the visual element of a man's inner life, I want to mention some common factors that make it harder for a man to stay pure in his thought life. Several organizations mention the HALT checklist: Hungry, Angry, Lonely, Tired.

If a man …
    is working long hours
    is out of sorts with the world (or his spouse)
    feels unappreciated
    feels like a failure as a provider or
    is far from home on a business trip—
his resolve may weaken. If our men are going to be the godly men most want to be, they will need support.

> Becky knew that when Jim was "hungry, angry, lonely, or tired" he was in greater danger. One night she felt a strong urge to pray for Jim, who was on a business trip to Las Vegas. She didn't know what was going on, but the urge was so strong that she called her pastor and asked him to pray also.
>
> The next day Jim called and told her: 'Last night, as I left the hotel to go out to dinner with the client, I noticed that it was "skinny-dipping" night. The "old" Jim made a mental note. In the taxi, after dropping the client off, having a drink poolside crossed my mind. However, I had the strongest impression that the taxi driver was praying for me. I came back to the hotel and went straight to my room and to bed.

Just as Becky praised the Lord for putting Jim in a Christian's taxi in the middle of Las Vegas, so are your prayers for your man powerful.

This week you have been making note of the visual temptations in our culture. It is not easy for our men. Besides making sure we are not a part of the problem and helping our man keep our eyes on us by watching our appearance, we can pray!

Searchlight
I hope you have read this chapter prayerfully, allowing God to give you peace rather than a knot in your stomach. God is a God of peace, after all. And He—like our husbands —loves us no matter what our imperfections are.

Use Galatians 6:1-3 to pray that God will keep you from temptations and help you be gentle in your response to the temptations that your husband faces.

Brothers, if someone is caught in any wrong-doing, you who are spiritual should restore such a person with a gentle spirit, watching out for yourselves so you won't be tempted also. Carry one another's burdens; in this way you will fulfill the law of Christ. For if anyone considers himself to be something when he is nothing, he is deceiving himself.
Galatians 6:1-3

If at any time you feel a need (like Becky in our HALT case study), you may want to read these Scriptures, perhaps going to your own Bible for more reflection. Fill in the blanks with your man's name as you pray these prayers for him. You may want to make a card out of each prayer and carry it with you as a prayer reminder as you go about your daily routine.

Psalm 19:12-13

Lord, keep _____ from willful sins. May lustful thoughts and images not rule over _____. Keep _____ blameless and innocent of great transgression.

Romans 7:15-25

Thank You, dear Lord, for rescuing _____ from the struggle with his sinful nature. May _____ be a slave to God's will. May _____ find delight in his inner being as he obeys. I pray that _____ will call on Christ for the power he needs.

2 Corinthians 10:4-5

Lord, give _____ divine power to demolish strongholds in his heart and mind. Strengthen _____ to demolish every argument and justification the Devil brings up. Give _____ the wisdom to take into captivity every thought and mental image in obedience to Christ.

Romans 8:5-6

I pray that _____ will live according to the Spirit and keep his mind on what the Spirit desires. Fill his mind with peace and life as it is controlled by the Spirit.

Keeper of the Visual Rolodex

Men are _____ , and women don't have any idea what that really means.

1. Even the most _____ man faces this struggle.

The issue is what he _____ ____ ____ with this involuntary temptation.
It is very _____ .

2. The image of the girl at Home Depot is _____ into his brain.
And her image can come back, even when he doesn't not want it.

They have to make the _____ between temptation and sin.

What is this culture like for men? _____ !

For Christian men, "taking every thought captive" is _____ _____ .

We can make his struggle worse by how we _____ .

We can make his struggle worse by the _____ we watch.

We can make his struggle worse by how we _____ .

One way a woman can support him is to care about her personal appearance.
It is emotionally important to a man that his wife _____ _____ _____
to take care of herself.

Words of encouragement

• They _____ _____ _____ as much as we do.

• This struggle has _____ ____ ____ with his love for us.

• They really do want our _____ .

week six

When I asked the very first test survey, of 10 men, whether they desired romance *for themselves,* every respondent chose to answer "yes, very much." I realized I had inadvertently been buying into the popular notion that men really don't care about romance. They do.

On the comprehensive survey that came later, 84 percent of respondents indicated that regardless of whether he was able to plan romantic events or whether his wife/girlfriend appreciated it, a man personally desires romance. This finding held true no matter the man's age or marital status.

As one representative survey-taker put it, "I wish my wife knew that I need romance, that I need touching and hugs as much as she does." I have to confess, the revelation that men actively enjoy and desire romance truly surprised me!

In the pages that follow, we will discover that men are not the unromantic clods they are sometimes portrayed to be. Instead, according to our research findings, most men feel that they are secret romantics who don't experience nearly as much intimacy with their wives as they would like.

The kicker is, guys often feel way out of their comfort zone when it comes to romance and to expressing their love for us. So we'll also talk this week about the tremendous power we have to change and strengthen this picture.

On the surveys we conducted, men had one final chance to express themselves by responding to this open-ended question:
What is the one thing that you wish she knew,
but you feel you can't explain to her or tell her?

Their answers? This week we'll take a look at some eye-opening responses. I think you are in for a surprise.

The changes in behavior and attitudes you have been trying to make do not become life-style patterns overnight. Even as you make small changes, you may find yourself after this study slipping back into earlier ways of thinking and acting.

If you desire additional encouragement, 10 Challenge Devotions are available for free download. To locate, go to *www.lifeway.com* and click on the Bible Studies for Women link to locate information about *For Women Only*. These short devotions can help you continue in your commitment to a new way of thinking and acting .

Ladies, I hope you feel that you have increased your knowledge, insights, and understandings into the inner lives of men, and most especially your man. I encourage you to continue focusing on God and on him as you conclude this study.

As God leads you in your relationship with your husband, future spouse, father, or son—make it a priority to *"use wisdom and understanding to establish your home; let good sense fill the rooms with priceless treasures" (Prov. 24:3-4. CEV).* May your "good sense" grow every day because it is based on new foundations. God bless you and your family as you delight in seeing your man become all that God intended for him to be.

Lightbulb

Most men enjoy romance and want to express their love to us—but hesitate because they doubt that they can succeed.

Weekly Challenge

It has been said that behind every great man is a great woman. Every day look for a seed of greatness in your man and write it in the margin of your book. Identify talents, skills, and abilities that you can affirm and ways you can support him.

Begin each day with a prayer that God will help you meet a new challenge. Practice every day. Continue to practice changes you are making from other Weekly Challenges.

"I wish that she knew how much I look up to her for ALL she is—intelligent, beautiful, capable, sexy, creative, generous, and kind. It seems that not a day passes when she doesn't feel insecure in one of these categories (or sometimes more than one). I wish that she had the confidence in herself that I have in her."

"I would like her to know every day that I love her with all my heart and would do anything it took to keep that love alive."

Can we really call men who express such sentiments "unromantic clods"? Men want romance; it just may look different. In Week 4, we talked a little about some redefinitions of romance. Do you remember that romance with your husband usually includes sex? And how if he invites you to go to a hardware store for the afternoon it could mean the same to him as a candlelight dinner would to you?

Our research shows that men really are romantic, but they struggle with issues of inadequacy in this area as well. Have you ever wondered why you only get a really romantic surprise every now and then? Keep reading!

Lightbulb
Most men are closet romantics.

Romance Looks Different to Men

As we were developing a test survey, I asked 50 men the question "Do you yourself desire romance?" One guy answered, "Yes, very much," adding in the margin, "but we have different definitions." I was intrigued by his comment, which became easier to understand once we obtained results from the main survey.

In those results, 60 percent of men said that they desired the candlelight dinner, cozy snuggle by the fire, or the sunset-on-the-beach type of romance. However, almost 40 percent said they preferred the "active" getting out and doing things with their wives— for example, hiking together, golfing together, or driving around and exploring.

> As Stephanie and Judy were taking their daily walk through the neighborhood, Stephanie complained that her husband was completely unromantic. She said he had invited her to go golfing with him and the guys last weekend!
>
> "I can't golf; he knows I'm a klutz!" moaned Stephanie. "What was he thinking? Whatever happened to dinner and a movie?"
>
> "That's nothing," said Judy. "Steve thinks that the perfect date is working both the Bass Pro Shop and The Home Depot into one evening. And if I'm lucky, we might swing by Waffle House on the way home. I'm thinking, *He got us a baby-sitter for this?*"

To you, are these men unromantic clods? ❑ yes ❑ no
What might be going through their minds as they attempted to be romantic with their wives?

Where is the "disconnect" in understanding and/or communication?

_____

Men view going out and doing things together as incredibly romantic. Here's a great insight from one husband: "Most married men don't want to abandon their wife to do guy things. They want to do 'guy things' with their wife. ... It's no different from when they were dating. For a guy, a big part of the thrill [then] was doing fun things together. The woman who is having fun with her husband is incredibly attractive."

"Playing" with their wives makes husbands feel close, loving, and intimate. It offers an escape from the ordinary, a time to focus on each other—all things that women also want from romance. Clearly, just as we want our husbands to love us in the way we need to be loved, so do our men want the same. It appears that the men we thought to be "unromantic clods" are romantics in hiding.

Why Men Don't Make a Move

When I've told women that they are probably married to a closet romantic, I usually hear this puzzled refrain: "Well, if they want to do romantic things, why don't they?"

Roadblock 1: He has failed or is afraid he will fail.

Apparently, many of us have overlooked the most basic stumbling block to his romantic initiative: self-doubt. Many men just feel clumsy in romance. As one guy said, "We do feel like clods sometimes. It's like trying to write with your left hand." When you factor in how performance-oriented men are, this self-doubt can translate into hesitation—or doing nothing at all—even if inside the man is yearning for romance.

Another man explained his performance anxieties this way: "The reason men practice sports so much is so they don't get embarrassed on the field—so they don't feel inadequate, but there's no way to practice romance. So, if they don't know how, they figure it's best not to even approach it and risk being seen as inadequate emotionally."

A man's willingness to take romantic risks may also be tied to how he is feeling about his job. A man who feels stressed and inadequate at work may feel particularly unable to risk feeling inadequate at home—in which case, it would be safer for him to do nothing.

> Chase spent weeks finding a special birthday present for Christa. After hours on the Internet and days of waiting, he finally had the perfect birthday present in his hands. He was totally jazzed as she unwrapped it.
>
> "Oh, thanks, sweetheart," Christa said sweetly and kissed him on the cheek. "Now, where are we going for dinner?"

How do you think Chase felt? _____

What will he likely do when another gift-giving occasion comes around?

_____

Next time, Chase will probably aim low and stay safe so he doesn't feel that his effort is wasted. As you can guess by now, if our men seem thoughtless or unromantic, they may actually be taking a safe course after what was (in their minds, at least) a painful romantic failure in the past.

How can you make sure your man is built up when he puts himself out to do something romantic? The same way you affirm him in all of his inner needs can encourage him to take the risk for romance.

But you, why do you criticize your brother? Or you, why do you look down on your brother? For we will all stand before the judgment seat of God.
Romans 14:10

How can each verse help you encourage your man in his romantic efforts?

Romans 14:10 _____

Romans 14:19 _____

Romans 15:1-2 _____

So then, we must pursue what promotes peace and what builds up one another.
Romans 14:19

Interestingly enough, scoring a romantic success can be just as paralyzing as failure. After a particularly spectacular birthday gift one year, I didn't get another "romantic" gift for the next three years. Not that I *minded*—I was just puzzled by the feast-or-famine trend where Jeff would sometimes go all-out to craft a romantic gift but at other times would sheepishly give me a gift certificate.

Now we who are strong have an obligation to bear the weaknesses of those without strength, and not to please ourselves. Each one of us must please his neighbor for his good, in order to build him up.
Romans 15:1-2

Finally, he confessed. "Guys are so competitive, and I'm even competitive with *myself*. I was sure that the next one wouldn't be as good, so there was no way to win." Thankfully, I was able to convince him that anything he put thought into made me feel special, which made it safe for him to try.

Roadblock 2: It's difficult for him to change gears.
Even working women may not appreciate how tough it is for a man to switch from the fast-paced, highly practical attitude of work to the tenderness of romance.

Jack entered the house through the front the door and took the stairs up to the bedroom. Dian heard his shoes hit the floor. She smiled to herself and checked the clock. Thirty minutes later, she checked her lipstick and took a tall glass of lemonade up to Jack.

What is your first reaction to this scene?

_____

Almost every man I talked to said he needs to somehow decompress after work before he can think about being a romantic, loving husband. If his wife can understand and give him that down time, he'll be happier and more available the rest of the evening.

How is Dian putting these verses into practice?
First Corinthians 13:4-5

_____

Luke 6:31

_____

"I wish I could make my wife understand that sometimes when I don't talk to her or act like a loving husband, it has nothing to do with how I feel about her," one man wrote. "I just sometimes need to be left alone with my own thoughts." These interviewees assured me that women shouldn't take this phenomenon personally; they just need space to relax and refresh for a while.

No doubt you are seeing that our men have deep emotional needs that require the same type of self-sacrificing love that we demand from them.

Fill in the blanks with words from the Word Bank, and so indicate your game plan the next time he redefines romance.
WORD BANK: record, kindness, don't envy, patient, do, don't act improperly, selfish,

Extend _____ by graciously accepting his invitation to go to the local hardware store—and having fun with him.
Choose to not be _____ with my time and do what he wants today.
Be _____ with his need to unwind after work.
Don't keep a _____ of how many times he doesn't do what I ask him when I am feeling romantic.
When he asks for sex, _____ as I would want him to _____ for me.

Is it dawning on you just how much power you have as a woman to change the entire romance picture? More than likely, you live with a motivated man who wants more romantic closeness, but is holding back or is frustrated.

 Searchlight
Read 1 Corinthians 10:23-24, NIV:
" 'Everything is permissible' —but not everything is beneficial.
'Everything is permissible'—but not everything is constructive.
Nobody should seek his own good, but the good of others."

"Don't I have a right to …?" Yes, you do.
"Shouldn't he …?" Yes, he should.
"Then why should I …?" Because that's what God wants.

The more we understand the men in our lives, the better we can support and love them in the way they need to be loved. In other words, this revelation is supposed to change and improve us. How are you doing?

We're in the final days of our journey together. It's time to share with you the single most important thing you need to know about the inner lives of men.

As I mentioned, at the end of every survey, I asked respondents one open-ended question that they could answer however they wanted. I figured: Give them a chance to vent. Let them say whatever they need to get off their chests. Wow! After the hundreds of answers rolled in, the top response was the most surprising of the survey.

Lightbulb

The top answer to the question *"What is the one thing that you wish your wife or girlfriend knew, but you feel you can't explain to her or tell her?"* is —drum roll, please—*"How much I love her."*

Drum Roll, Please

I was stunned. Here was a perfect opportunity for men to share all those things they wished their mate would work on. But far and away, the largest number of those responding chose to use the space to say they wished their wife knew "How much I really do love her" (or the cousin statement that there is nothing he couldn't share with his girlfriend). Out of the infinite number of topics they *could* have mentioned, to have 32 percent of the men give the same message is astounding … and wonderful.

One man surveyed seemed to capture perfectly the way many men feel about the women in their lives, even if there *are* things in the relationship that need work. He answered that he wished his wife knew "how important some things are to me that I won't mention because she's more important to me than all those other things."

Men want to show us how much they love us and long for their women to understand what is going on inside them, even though they sometimes can't explain it well. More than once I have seen men tear up as they are moved by the thought that their wives might be able or desirous to truly understand them.

Do you ever doubt whether your man loves you? Do you find yourself saying, "If he loved me, he would or he wouldn't …?"

Spotlight

Are there ways he might be trying to express his love to you that you are not even recognizing?

We've talked a lot in this study about all those things your man may need, but intentionally haven't dealt with what you and I need. What we need, of course, is to feel his love. And if he is like most men, he really does long to show it to you.

Men's hearts are so tender toward their wives, but guys often feel that they cannot show their true emotions. When I began to understand this, I realized how many times Jeff had cautiously opened himself up only to have me nonchalantly (and certainly unknowingly) launch a dart into his heart.

Encourage Him

Although a wife's appreciation is always needed, it is especially critical when the man is outside his comfort zone—which, when it comes to romance, is probably the case for half the male population. One man was blunt:

> "Encourage me and affirm my efforts, and I'll run through a brick wall to please you. Don't just assume that I know you're pleased. I'm way outside my comfort zone. I'm willing to be a fool for you, but just tell me that I did good. And give me sex. That helps too."

> Marcos knew that Sylvia had been working really hard on her big project. She came home every day exhausted. Tonight he would be ready. The table was set. He lit the candles when he heard her car. Soft music played in the background, and his marinara sauce bubbled on the stove. Everything was perfect as they started the meal. Suddenly, Sylvia hopped up, still chatting away about the challenges of the day.

> She looked through the cupboard, grabbed the oregano, and peppered her pasta with it. When she took a bite and looked up, she knew by the look on Marcos's face that something was terribly awry.

What do you think Marcos was feeling? What was Sylvia's intent?

_____

Many men view taking romantic initiative as a huge risk—a risk of "being humiliated." It hardly seems fair but the most innocent gesture on our part can be interpreted as, "My performance was evaluated and found lacking." Even if we don't mean to criticize, a man can feel inadequate if we don't make an effort to show appreciation.

Read Romans 14:13. Check actions you could take that would not create a stumbling block.
- ❏ Pay attention to his attempts to be romantic.
- ❏ Don't worry about how he might take what I say.
- ❏ Ask yourself, _Would I want him to say or do this to me?_
- ❏ Say exactly what you think any time.
- ❏ Use your best manners, just as you would for a visitor.
- ❏ Make a joke about his attempt at romance.
- ❏ Others of your own: _____

Therefore, let us no longer criticize one another, but instead decide not to put a stumbling block or pitfall in your brother's way.
Romans 14:13

Prove to your man that romance is not a risk! When he makes an effort, it's _your_ responsibility—and your joy—to demonstrate how much it was appreciated. Will you have to put some thought into it? Yes. Is it worth it? No question.

Entice Him

Just as men want to be encouraged, so do they also want to be enticed. Many men have told me that whether it is in work or in romance, they are always looking for some new conquest, something to "catch."

A key element, then, in keeping romance alive is to keep giving our romance-loving husbands something to conquer. Keep the relationship fresh—give him something to pursue. Go hiking with him. Play golf with him. Give him space when he needs it—and intimate attention when he needs that! Make yourself the kind of friend and lover he constantly wants to pursue.

Even when a man *isn't* outside his comfort zone, he can become frustrated when we don't want to "go outside and play" when the opportunity arises. So next time he suggests something, don't tell him you really need to vacuum the house. Give him his version of a candlelight dinner, and enjoy your romantic time together!

The Hope of Ordinary Men

One man provided great encouragement to every woman out there who wants to support her man in becoming all God intends him to be. He said,

> "It is so true, that behind every great man is a great woman. There are a lot of men out there who are mediocre, simply because their wives will not support them and bring them to greatness. And there are a lot of mediocre men who are destined to become great men—who *are becoming* great men—because their wives love and support them."

Your last Weekly Challenge is to take the first steps to making your man great! Each day, look for a seed of greatness in your man and write it in the margin. Identify talents, skills, and abilities that you can affirm and ways you can support him. By now, you should have a list of things you can affirm about your man. You can add to that list how much he adores you. Here are a few of the loving comments written in the survey.

Read these comments to yourself, hearing them in your man's voice.
"I wish she knew that …"
❏ "I love her more than she thinks I do."
❏ "I will love her no matter what."
❏ "She is the most important thing in life."
❏ "She truly is the light of my life."
❏ "We have been together a long time and I hope she knows I will always love her."

Spotlight

Put yourself in these men's shoes. How would it feel to have this much love and not feel able to express it? Or to feel that it has not been understood?

_____

_____

_____

Day-to-day life has a way of dimming the fires of passion. I hope that hearing how much he really does care has warmed your heart. This is a vital part of a week full of words for your heart.

Searchlight

Perhaps you are feeling overwhelmed. Changing the way we look at our men and then deciding what that means to our behavior takes a lot of commitment and a lot of energy.

Read Romans 8:37 aloud several times. Emphasize different words each time. Soak in the victory that can be yours through the Lord. He loves you, too! Spend some moments in praise to God.

No, in all these things we are more than conquerors through him who loved us.
Romans 8:37, NIV

Interestingly enough, he does love you! The research proves it! He wants the best for you, but he feels he has a hard time getting the point across to us. And romance? Too much risk.

Once again we see how vulnerable our men really are and what an opportunity we have to make them feel safe.

Lightbulb

When he says, "I love you," he means it, and when he feels like "number one," he knows you love him back.

"But He ..."

Let me ask you this: Do you have trouble believing that he has goodwill toward you? When things don't go our way or hard times come, it is easy to assume our man is acting against us on purpose. When you are hurt, you feel he doesn't love you. Because your deep need is to feel his love, you are quick to suspect that he is withholding that very thing.

> It was very important to Raul that Maria be at home when the children came home from school. Maria had grown up as a latchkey kid, and she trusted her kids to behave for the few minutes it might take her to run an extra errand on the way home from her job, but Raul was adamant. Maria would change jobs or manage to be at home when the bus came. Maria was furious.

What would you say Maria was thinking?

_____

At first read, what was your reaction to this scenario? Be honest.

_____

Often when there is a conflict, women feel that what their husbands are demanding is designed to make their lives miserable. "Men just want to get their way and be the boss." "He likes telling me what to do." "Why can't he see how much effort that is for me?"

He Really Loves You

Here are a few more heartfelt answers from the men surveyed. "I want her to know ...
- "How much I truly do care for and love her and the kids."
- "How much she means to me."
- "How great a person I think she is."
- "I am very happy with my wife. ... She may not be the perfect woman, but she is the perfect woman for me."
- "After so many years, I hope my wife knows that she is the best hope in my life. We don't have everything that we desire material-wise, but there is so much more to life than that. I hope my wife knows that I love her and cherish our friendship, forever."

Remember that the men writing these inspiring words of love may not look very romantic. They aren't doing everything just perfectly, but you are privileged to hear what is found in the depths of their hearts. And you know what? This is just what God expects of them. Read Ephesians 5:28-29 in the margin. (No, you can't hold this over his head. This is still about you and the inner life of your husband!)

With what kind of love does God love the church? Now read these Scriptures from *The Message* and draw a line from the verse to the characteristic of love.

constant   Romans 5:8
self-sacrificing   Philippians 2:3
selfless   Jeremiah 31:3

If your man is seeking to honor God and you, then he loves you just as God loves the church. What does that look like? One man responded to the survey this way: "I love her and only her. It doesn't matter that our relationship isn't perfect—my love for her is so deep that nothing could break it."

Since this study is all about what your husband thinks and feels, and what you need to do as a result, why reprint verses that talk about how your *man* should love *you*? First, because my research has shown that this is how most men feel, even if they also feel they aren't doing a very good job of showing it. Second, because it has become so clear that if a wife will show her husband unconditional respect and affirm and support him as the helpmate God intended her to be, her husband will usually come to show love to her as he should.

This is God's plan. And I have heard story after story of it happening just this way! First, let me ask you, do you believe the survey responses of those men? If you do believe that your man loves you, then you can know that the beat of his heart is not to hurt you.

Read Romans 13:10 and fill in the blank to find an encouraging description of love.

"Love does _____ _____ to a neighbor. Love, therefore, is the fulfillment of the law."

He may disappoint you, he may not do everything right, he may struggle with issues, and he may not do things the way you think he should; but chances are good that what your man does and says is not meant to harm you.

Spotlight
Does knowing of this love change how you see your man? Do you love him?

_____

_____

_____

In the same way, husbands should love their wives as their own bodies. He who loves his wife loves himself. For no one ever hates his own flesh, but provides and cares for it, just as Christ does for the church.
Ephesians 5:28-29

I've never quit loving you and never will. Expect love, love, and more love!
Jeremiah 31:3,
The Message

But God put his love on the line for us by offering his son in sacrificial death while we were of no use whatever to him.
Romans 5:8,
The Message

Think of yourselves the way Christ Jesus thought of himself. He had equal status with God but didn't think so much of himself that he had to cling to the advantages of that status no matter what.
Philippians 2:3,
The Message

Love does no wrong to a neighbor. Love, therefore, is the fulfillment of the law.
Romans 13:10

If so, then let's look at a few more ways you can make sure that your words and actions don't harm or wrong him. You have nothing to lose and everything to gain by supporting your man—including in romance.

Keep Him Number One

One of the most common concerns I heard is that we may unconsciously prioritize our kids over our husband. On the survey, several men expressed concern that "she spends too much time doting on the children" and not enough time doting on the relationship. Martha and Mary were sisters, and they had opened their home to Jesus. As the home-maker, Martha was totally psyched with her duties as hostess. Mary's focus was on Jesus. She saw her opportunity to learn from Him, and she took her place at His feet. The many things to be done so claimed Martha's attention that she lost it. "Lord, don't you care that my sister has left me to serve alone?"

"… but one thing is necessary. Mary has made the right choice, and it will not be taken away from her."
Luke 10:42

Check the statement that best makes Jesus' point in Luke 10:42.
- ❏ Martha, don't be so busy that you miss what is really important.
- ❏ Martha, don't waste your time. What you are doing is not important.

Your romance with your husband is the most important relationship you have. Do you let other responsibilities come before him? It is easy to think that he understands or that he will still be there when everything else is done.

Caution:
Love will never allow you to be physically or verbally abused. If your man struggles with issues that cause him to hurt you, then seek help. God does not expect you to sit silently and let someone cause physical or mental harm to you or your family.

A man with active children commented, "It's considered a Christian thing to do, to be with the kids all the time. But for me as a man, there is a sense of 'I've lost my wife.' It could sound selfish, but it's not. And it's not too healthy for the kids either." One man said, "It's not just kids that steal a wife. It's the whole 'to do' list. Even helping others can get in the way."

These men just want more quality, romantic time with their wives. What an irony, considering that most women pine for the same thing! We have a tremendous opportunity to start over with our men—and in the process, rediscover the delight of the mutual pursuit.

Spotlight

What would your husband say about your priorities? Has he given you any signals that he would like to spend more time with you alone?

_____

_____

_____

Tell Harry What Sally Needs

Men love their wives, but they do not always feel that they can clearly communicate when it comes to love and romance issues. Several men suggested that since they can't read your mind, it is fine to drop hints about those romantic things you'd like to do as long as they truly are hints, not directives.

If you saw the 1989 classic movie *When Harry Met Sally*, then you'll remember how the issue of cuddling emerged between the two main characters. Because cuddling tends to be more important to women like Sally than to guys like Harry, a little patient reeducation may be in order. This applies to anything you find particularly romantic that *he* doesn't get.

"Help me understand why it's so important to you," one man suggested. "Help me see that as I romance you in *your* way, you'll be more motivated to romance me in *my* way." One husband's response to the cuddling example was, "Men can learn to enjoy a time of closeness after sex. In this case, it is definitely in our best interest to understand why it matters so much to you!"

This approach isn't a hurtful, withholding-based model. Rather, it is learning to give what the other person needs and enjoying the resulting God-ordained fruits of that selflessness.

Searchlight

We're approaching the end of our time together but hopefully not the end of our continuing journey in building godly relationships. Today let's read and respond to 1 Corinthians 13:4-7 in *The Message*.

> *Love never gives up.*
> *Love cares more for others than for self.*
> *Love doesn't want what it doesn't have.*
>
> *Love doesn't strut,*
> *Doesn't have a swelled head,*
> *Doesn't force itself on others,*
> *Isn't always "me first,"*
> *Doesn't fly off the handle,*
> *Doesn't keep score of the sins of others,*
> *Doesn't revel when others grovel,*
> *Takes pleasure in the flowering of truth,*
> *Puts up with anything,*
>
> *Trusts God always,*
> *Always look for the best,*
> *Never looks back,*
> *But keeps going to the end.*

Underline the parts of this look at love that could help you seek your man's interests in romance rather than your own.

Draw a large heart over this passage.
The Lord is the only one who can provide you with this kind of *agape* love. Seek His face each and every day.

Circle the parts that are hardest for you.
Ask the Lord to strengthen you, change you, guide you so that you will be able to put that kind of love into action.

Draw a box around the last four lines.
Continue to look for the best in your man. Forgive and forget the past. Keep going in the knowledge you have gained. Pray, telling God that you are trusting Him to "complete the good work" He has begun in you and your man.

May I pray for you today? Let me base my prayer on Philippians 1:3-7 (HCSB).

I give thanks to my God for every remembrance of you,
always praying with joy for all of you.
From the first day of this study
you have been my partner in the gospel.
Lord, I trust You to complete the good work
I know You have started in each woman.
Fill each one with love that never gives up.
It is right for me to think this way
about all of you,
because I have you in my heart.
In Jesus' name, I pray.
Amen.

"My wife expects great things from me," one man commented, "even though I'm a pretty ordinary guy really. She looks at me like I'm a genius in my field. She respects me in public and affirms me in private. I love her. And like all men, I want to live up to her expectations."

He makes a terrific point: We have tremendous power in the lives of our men.

Lightbulb
A woman has tremendous power for good or evil in the life of her man.

The Power of a Woman In Love
If you've been disappointed in your relationship with your man and have pushed and prodded to no effect, you've probably realized that nagging doesn't work. Yet, in many cases, we do hold the key to a wonderful relationship with our men.

As you know by now, a woman is to respect her husband (see Eph. 5:33). I hope by now that you have a entirely new vision of what that means in all the elements of a man's inner life. The key to a quality relationship with your man is so simple: do it God's way.

You may have struggled with this understanding over these weeks. But as Romans 8:37, our memory verse this week, reminds us, *"No, in all these things we are more than conquerors through him who loved us."* Our Lord, as always, is our perfect example. Plus, He gives us the perfect method to carry out His command.

Read 1 John 3:16 and fill in the blanks:

Because Christ _____ _____ _____ _____ for us,

we should _____ _____ _____ _____ for our brothers.

This is how we have come to know love: He laid down His life for us. We should also lay down our lives for our brothers.
1 John 3:16

Circle any form of the word *love* in these verses.
First John 4:10-11:
"Love consists in this: not that we loved God, but that He loved us and sent His Son to be the propitiation for our sins. Dear friends, if God loved us in this way, we also must love one another."
First John 4:21:
"And we have this command from Him: the one who loves God must also love his brother."
First John 2:3,5:
"This is how we are sure that we have come to know Him: by keeping His command. . . . But whoever keeps His word, truly in him the love of God is perfected."

Mark these statements as true *(T)* or false *(F)* based on these verses.
___ Look out for yourself and God will look out for everyone else.
___ Because of God's great love for you, spend yourself loving others.
___ If we love God, we will try to do things His way.
___ I have to be perfect to do things the way God wants.
___ God can love in and through me when I obey His commands.

Loving God's way will lead you to meet your man's needs the way he needs them to be met. While a popular song lyric tells us "all you need is love," love is no good unless it is received, and it can't be received if it does not meet the needs of the beloved. You have to choose to put aside, if for just a little bit, your needs and wants.

Created to Cleave

Genesis 2:24 is often quoted (and frequently from the poetic King James Version of the Bible) at marriage ceremonies. This is where we find God's plan for marriage: a man leaves his family and cleaves to his wife, and the two become one.

It is a two-step process. The couple has to leave their previous individual lives. Leaving is more than changing addresses. You may have to leave your way of doing things or your ideas of what works best. You may have to leave your notion of what men are like.

Then, the couple has to cleave. Think of it this way: "...In the eyes of God, cleaving means wholehearted commitment, first of all spiritual, but spilling into every area of our being. So that the cleaving is also intellectual, emotional, and physical. It means that you will have unceasing opportunity to cleave to your partner even in the smallest details of life."[1]

Let me ask you a question. Do you feel more able intellectually, emotionally, and maybe even physically to make the most of every opportunity to support your man in the little details of his inner life? Putting into practice what God has revealed to you will take commitment. Your effort to support him in the smallest thing will make a huge difference. It really is all about the details.

In fact, cleaving can be summed up this way: "All must be put into proper perspective. Whatever is important to you in this life should be less important than your marriage."[2] As you have turned the Spotlight on your man and the Searchlight into your own heart, you have had to test some actions, attitudes, and words.

In the weeks ahead, you might want to consider these questions offered by Dr. Wheat as you go forward in your new understanding of your husband. Before you speak, act, or react, ask yourself: *Will this draw us closer or drive us part? Will it build our relationship or tear it down? Will it bring about a positive response or a negative response? Does it express my love and loyalty to my partner, or does it reveal my self-centered individualism?* [3]

What a Summary!

You've had a chance to enjoy several responses to the survey question. The top-five concerns the men expressed are in the adjacent column. Do they look familiar?

Compare the top-five responses to the seven revelations that are summarized on page 159. Write in the blanks the three that are missing.

_____

_____

_____

The Envelope, Please

The top 5 answers to the open-ended survey question:

#5. 10 percent said: "I need her to understand my burden to provide, how draining my job is."

#4. 10 percent said: "I need more sex."

#3. 15 percent said: "I need more respect, in private and public."

#2. 18 percent said: "I wish she'd make more of an effort to take care of herself."

#1. 32 percent said: "I wish she knew how much I love her."

If you identified "men are insecure," "men are visual," and "men enjoy romance" as the missing revelations, then you're right on target. Good work!

Put a check beside the revelation or survey answer(s) in the box that you feel your man would most want you to know.

We have been talking about elements related to the inner lives of men that we women just do not get. As it turns out, what they want most us to know is what they don't know how to tell us. The Lightbulb experiences you have been having are meant to help you have the good sense to see behind those strong, hard (sometimes unshaven) faces to the vulnerable, sensitive souls inside—and then to "lay down" your life for them.

Use Your Good Sense

"A beautiful woman who rejects good sense is like a gold ring in a pig's snout" (Prov. 11:22). Forgive me, I couldn't resist this delightful, but dramatic saying. Your attractiveness as a woman shines through when you use good sense. To live without using the understanding and wisdom that God has given you these weeks would be as inconsistent and unbecoming as a gold ring in a pig's snout.

In 1 Samuel we find the story of a woman in a trying situation who knew how to use her good sense. Abigail was married to a difficult man, Nabal. When she heard that Nabal had insulted David and his men, she knew she had to do something. She gathered an array of gifts and set out to find David. With charm and insight, she calmed David's vengeful spirit and saved the day for her husband, his men, and her family.

Read 1 Samuel 25:32-35. According to verse 33, what quality did David praise in Abigail?

_____

Abigail used her wisdom and discretion to make the best of an unfortunate situation.

Spotlight
What discernment has God given you during these weeks?

_____

Do you remember another proverb, the one that opened our time together? *"Use wisdom and understanding to establish your home; let good sense fill the rooms with priceless treasures. Wisdom brings strength, and knowledge gives power"* (Prov. 24:3-4, CEV).

How are you filling your rooms with priceless treasures?

_____

You have been gaining wisdom and knowledge. Now, look at the following scenarios, and use your newfound "good sense" to turn these situations around.

LinChi's husband had worked late every night this week. When he came home Friday evening, she was fuming. Before Lee put his briefcase down, she blurted out, "Don't you care about us at all?"

What did LinChi not get?

_____

What lightbulb needs to come on for LinChi?

_____

How could she have reacted differently?

_____

Ed jammed his fist into the pillow. Third "no" this week! *You would think I could be a little more interesting to Carol than that book!* he thought grimly. *Oh, great,* he remembered, *the Jackson meeting is in the morning. I'm going be in some shape tomorrow.*

What did Carol not get?

_____

What lightbulb needs to come on for Carol?

_____

How could she have reacted differently?

_____

"You should have seen the water shooting out everywhere!" Kathy Lynn cackled. "I told James he should never have tried to fix that sink all by himself!"

What did Kathy Lynn not get?

_____

What lightbulb needs to come on for Kathy Lynn?

_____

How could she have reacted differently?

_____

Don sighed through clinched teeth. He wished there were another route home. "Oh, look," said Carrie, "The hot sign is on at the donut shop. Pull in before we pick up Megan at daycare."

What did Carrie not get?

_____

What lightbulb needs to come on for Carrie?

_____

How could she have reacted differently?

_____

Searchlight

"Use wisdom and understanding to establish your home; let good sense fill the rooms with priceless treasures. Wisdom brings strength, and knowledge gives power." Thank the Lord for the wisdom and knowledge you have gained. Ask Him for guidance in areas in which you might still feel like you need a little more discretion.

Some of us may be challenged by what we have learned in these pages. These realities may not fit our idealistic or politically correct views of men. But just as we have discussed the difficult choices we expect our men to make, we must make our own hard decisions. We can remain behind safe, carefully constructed viewpoints about our men, or we can step out in courage to face the truth—and all that it means for what we must become.

Let us accept this call to maturity and receive this invitation for our generation to become the strong, gentle, godly women our men need. If we are willing to be molded by His hands, the Lord will shower us, our men, and our relationships with abundance. That is the way He works. He made us for each other. He is the Author of love.

Lightbulb

A man can be propelled into the greatness to which God is calling him by a woman who meets his inner needs.

Our Journey Continues

I am fascinated by this journey to explore the inner wiring of men. Notice the present tense verb. I am still on this journey with you! Although I make many mistakes in my relationship with my husband—and will continue to!—finally grasping these things has helped me to better appreciate and support him in the way that he needs.

> A phone call came in this week from a woman who said God had thoroughly challenged her as she read *For Women Only: What You Need to Know About the Inner Lives of Men.* "The Lord showed me that I needed to grow up," she said. "For years I focused on how Phil didn't measure up to or meet my expectations, but now I'm concentrating on fixing the lady in the mirror. That'll take two lifetimes before I'll even have time to get to his problems!"
>
> The woman went on to share how pleasantly surprised her husband was at her new attitude—and how much he was enjoying an accusation-free environment for the first time in 20 years.

By becoming more of what my husband needs, I can propel him into the greatness to which God is calling him. I become a colaborer with God in his life and not a stumbling block interested in just my way. I trust that lightbulb has come on for you as well.

Accepting the Call to Maturity

"Love must be sincere. Hate what is evil; cling to what is good. Be devoted to one another in brotherly love. Honor one another about yourselves" (Rom. 12:9-10, NIV). Following are some e-mails I have received and other stories from women who are growing up, beginning to forsake selfishness, and learning to honor their spouses before themselves.

Take advantage of the spaces provided to begin writing your own stories in response to these situations and Scriptures, even though more experiences have yet to be recorded.

These are the type of e-mails that frequently brighten my day:

"Shaunti, your book has opened the door to my husband's mind, and I now see how my responses can make or break him. We have always had a blessed marriage, but now I really get it. We are all part of God's marvelous creation and IT IS GOOD!"

"Thank you, Shaunti, for your gentle challenge to shake off my old mind-sets and the lies I have believed about men. I bought your book last Christmas and wrote down my goal of becoming a better wife, but it was this Christmas when I got the greatest gift of all. My husband took my hands in his and said, 'Baby, you really have become a better wife this year.' God bless you for these truths!"

What's your story?

_____

_____

_____

Cindy realized that she treated everyone else with respect. She chose her words carefully, gave the other person the benefit of the doubt, and listened to their opinions—except when it came to her husband.

Luanne enjoyed being the life of the party. People loved hearing her stories. Then she realized that most of her anecdotes were about her husband, Andrew.

What's your story?

_____

_____

_____

"Never be lacking in zeal, but keep your spiritual fervor, serving the Lord. Be joyful in hope, patient in affliction, faithful in prayer. Share with God's people who are in need. Practice hospitality" (Rom. 12:11-13, NIV).

Wanda championed prayer in the missions group at church. She organized prayer luncheons and handed out prayer calendars. Then, she realized that her husband needed her daily prayers to face all the burdens of being a man.

Richard had been out of a job for months. Deborah's patience had long ago given way to irritation and was bordering on disgust. Then, she realized that she had been adding to his feelings of inadequacy.

What's your story?

_____

_____

_____

"Bless those who persecute you; bless and do not curse. Rejoice with those who rejoice; mourn with those who mourn. Live in harmony with one another. Do not be proud, but be willing to associate with people of low position. Do not be conceited" (Rom. 12:14-15, NIV).

What's your story?

_____

_____

_____

"Do not repay anyone evil for evil. Be careful to do what is right in the eyes of everybody. If it is possible as far as it depends on you, live at peace with everyone. Do not take revenge, my friends, but leave room for God's wrath, for it is written: It is mine to avenge I will repay, says the Lord'" (Rom. 12:17-19, NIV).

What's your story?

_____

_____

_____

Searchlight

The woman who understands the inner life of men will see her husband in a new light. She will assume the best about him and find ways to show her respect for him as a man. She affirms him so that he goes out into the world with confidence. She encourages and appreciates him as a provider. She rewards him with the kind of sexual desire that leaves him no doubt of her love.

Now when she sees him catch a glimpse of a pretty woman, she prays. She has learned to find interesting things on their trips to the hardware store and to eat lumpy oatmeal on a breakfast tray with as much passion as steak and shrimp by candlelight. She couldn't be happier. Her man is living up to her expectations in ways she never imagined!

As you go forward from this study, may your house be filled with similar precious treasures. May what you have discovered encourage you to move ahead in hope, in confidence, and in peace.

In Matthew 6, Jesus taught His disciples (then and now) how to pray. I have used this Model Prayer as a pattern for prayer for the woman who understands the intricate details of the way God has created men.

I leave these thoughts with you—as both a prayer for myself and for you.

My Father in heaven,
Your are holy and wondrous.
I have faith that my relationships can be all that You want them to be.
Lord, today give me the insight, wisdom, grace, and love
to be the woman You want me to be.
Forgive me where I failed yesterday and help me to
forgive my mate his failings.

Help me not to be tempted by selfishness, anger, loneliness, pride, or revenge.
Protect my mind, my heart, and my tongue.
Help me to reflect Your glory in everything I do or say.
Amen.

The Power of a Woman in Love

Men really do desire _____ with their wives.

1. Guys often feel _____ at romance so sometimes don't take the risk.

   Do you realize what this means? Whether or not they are romantic may be up to _____ .

2. We often miss their _____ for romance.

   If it's romance to him, why not learn to _____ it?

They also feel _____ in telling us how much they love us, how deeply they care about us.

Do you have a sense of the _____ God has given you, to build up or tear down?

Are you willing to pray this prayer:

_____ my mind, _____ my eyes, _____ me things I didn't even know I needed to see about my man. God is doing a great work in you and in your man.

Lord, we do want our rooms
to be filled with precious and priceless treasures.
We want our homes
to have love and laughter around every corner.

We know You have given us awesome responsbility
in the lives of the men around us.
Help us, through Your Holy Spirit, to continue to practice
the new insights You have given us.

Continue to open our eyes and to give us
knowledge, understanding, wisdom, and good sense
in building our homes and our relationships.
We love You, and we trust You , and we thank You.
Amen.

Now that my eyes have been opened to my man's inner life, I will

1. Assume the best about him as a man made in God's image, and do my part to understand his unique desires and needs.

2. Choose to trust him and join the adventure, even when he's driving in circles and won't ask for directions.

3. Catch myself before I complain about him to others, and brag on him instead.

4. Every day, find something he's really good at and then affirm him in that area.

5. Notice how he feels about providing, and thank him for his commitment.

6. Recognize that my husband doesn't just want more sex; he also needs to feel that I *desire* and *enjoy* him sexually.

7. Pray daily for him in our visually distracting culture, and support and appreciate his efforts to keep his thought life pure.

8. Understand that he may be proposing a romantic rendezvous when he says, "Hey, honey—wanna go to The Home Depot with me?"

9. Make sure he knows I take my appearance seriously, and that he sees me making an effort to take care of myself for him.

10. Embrace his efforts to tell me how much he loves me—in whatever way he conveys that best—and let him know that I believe him.

_____   _____

(signature)   (date)

SEVEN SURPRISING REVELATIONS

1. Men want respect even more than love.
2. Even confident-seeming men secretly doubt themselves.
3. He feels like it's his job to provide for the family even if you do also.
4. A husband wants to feel desired by his wife.
5. Even the most devoted husband has visual temptation.
6. Men enjoy romance but doubt they can succeed.
7. When you make an effort to take care of yourself, he feels cared for.

Permission is granted to duplicate this page for FWO Bible study groups.

The statistical results and interviews with men related to the seven surprising revelations are based on the research that is the basis of *For Women Only: What You Need to Know About the Inner Lives of Men* (Multonomah). In some cases, comments by the men who had been interviewed were edited to fit the space.

The entire research survey is available to read at *www.4-womenonly.com*. Other elements (for example, the follow-up survey of churchgoers and written responses to the question "What is the one most important thing you wish your wife knew?") are also on this site.

Week 1
Day 1
1. Respect as "to refrain from interfering with": *http://www.m-w.com/cgi-bin/dictionary*.

2. Husbands and wives may want to explore further the love-respect message and principles of communication. The content in the "newcomers" section of Dr. Emerson Eggerich's Web site, *www.loveandrespect. com*, may be especially helpful.

Week 2
Introduction:
The Star Trek reference is from *Star Trek: The Next Generation* by Gene Roddenberry, episode #260, "Attached." The exact quotes were tracked down by Steve Krutzler, editor, *www.TrekWeb.com*.

Day 2:
1. Francis Maguire, *You're the Greatest! How Validated Employees Can Impact Your Bottom Line* (Germantown, TN: Saltillo Press, 2001), 210-11.

Day 3:
2. Willard F. Harley, Jr., *His Needs Her Needs* (Grand Rapids, MI: Fleming H. Revell, 1986), 152.

Day 4:
3. Ed Wheat, *Intended for Pleasure* (Grand Rapids, MI: Fleming H. Revell, 1997), 125.
4. Willard F. Harley, Jr., *His Needs Her Needs* (Grand Rapids, MI: Fleming H. Revell, 1986), 124.

Week 3
Day 4
1. Merrill Unger, *Unger's Bible Dictionary* (Chicago, IL: Moody Press, 1966), 219.

2. W. E. Vine, *Expanded Vine's Expository Dictionary of New Testament Words* (Minneapolis, MN: Bethany House Publishers, 1984), 226.

3. Willard F. Harley, Jr., *His Needs Her Needs* (Grand Rapids, MI: Fleming H. Revell, 1986), 124.

Day 5:
The Lord of the Rings: The Return of the King, 2003, New Line Studios, directed by Peter Jackson; cast, Elijah Wood, Sean Astin; based on the novel by J. R. R. Tolkien.

Week 4
Day 1:
1. Ed Wheat, *Love Life for Every Married Couple* (Grand Rapids, MI: Zondervan Publishing House, 1980), 20. Out of print.

Day 4:
The illustrations provided by "Gail" are based on "Not Tonight, Dear…" by Jill Eggleton Brett, *Today's Christian Woman*, 24, no. 2 (March/April 2002): 68.

Day 5:
2. Ed Wheat, *Love Life for Every Married Couple* (Grand Rapids, MI: Zondervan Publishing House, 1980), 25.

Week 6
Day 4:
1. Ed Wheat, *Love Life for Every Married Couple* (Grand Rapids, MI: Zondervan Publishing House, 1980), 30-31.
2. Wheat, *Love Life*, 28.
3. Wheat, *Love Life*, 31.

The For Women Only Covenant is taken from *For Women Only: Discussion Guide* by Shaunti Feldhahn with Lisa A. Rice (Sisters, OR: Multnomah Publishers, 2005), 48.

Leader Guide

This leader guide will help you facilitate seven one-hour sessions (including an introductory session) of *For Women Only: The Bible Study*. The *For Women Only Leader Kit* (ISBN 1-4158-3496-2) includes two DVDs and a member book. In 20- to 30-minute video teaching segments, Shaunti helps women apply what they are learning in their home study. Ladies will also hear from a men's focus group led by Shaunti's husband, Jeff.

About the Study
For Women Only: The Bible Study may attract women in your community who are not part of any church. The study's appeal is in both the message (stronger marriages/relationships) and also the scriptural principles and devotional style. Be aware of women who may not be Christians or who are unaccustomed to a church environment. Help them feel a part of the group by introducing them to one another.

You can intentionally try to reach this group by meeting in a home or other relaxed setting. Work with your women's ministry or other leaders.

Format for the Sessions
Teaching plans are based on a one-hour schedule, with content for expanding the session and ideas for singles. Each session includes these elements:

Welcome and opening remarks; video (25 min.)
Use the opening five minutes to help all women feel welcome. Ask whether they have questions from the homework. Some questions may be clarified by Shaunti in the video, since the video wraps up what women studied the previous week. The leader can use a Video Reflection for emphasis or summary.

Show the video and direct women to complete the viewer guide, located at the end of each week's readings. Answers for the leader are on page 174.

Discussion (20 min.)
As a total group or through small-group assignments if your group is larger, allow women to share insights, questions, and possible solutions. Sometimes a question represents one of the homework days, but not always. As leader, be responsible for providing any other information your group needs.

Debrief and conclude (10-15 min.)
Bring small groups back together if needed. Debrief assignments and close with prayer. Briefly overview the coming week's homework and Weekly Challenge.

Basic
1 hour (55-60 min.)
Welcome and opening remarks	5 min.
Video viewing	20-25 min.
Small-group discussion	20 min.
Debrief and conclude	10 min.

• *Includes prayer*

Expanded
1 1/2 hours (90 min.)
Welcome and opening remarks	10 min.
Video viewing	20-25 min.
Small-group discussion	35 min.
• *Use "If you have more time" options*	
Debrief and conclude	10-20 min.

• *Includes prayer*
• *Show bonus material on DVD*

Expanded
2 hours (120 min.)
Welcome and opening remarks	15 min.
Video viewing	20-25 min.
Break into small groups	5 min.
Small-group discussion	40 min.
• *Use "If you have more time" options*	
Refreshments/fellowship	15 min.
Debrief and conclude	15-20 min.

• *Includes prayer*
• *Show bonus material on DVD*

Stay together for the welcome and video viewing; discuss assignments as smaller groups; and debrief and conclude with everyone together.

If you expect a large number, also enlist a facilitator for every 7-12 women. In a large room such as a fellowship hall, you can group women at round tables for easy sharing and ask someone at each table to guide the discussion.

Ideally, three to five women share together. In general, the fewer people, the greater the chance that everyone will feel comfortable enough to share.

Preparing for This Study
❑ First and foremost, prepare your heart and mind. Pray for the women who will be involved and for the relationships they represent. Familiarize yourself with the workbook and DVDs, activities, and Scriptures.

❏ In advance order the number of books you anticipate needing, to distribute at the Introductory Session. Know that some women who attend the Introductory Session have not yet decided to participate.

❏ Set the date and time for sessions. Be sure to check the church calendar if planned for a church setting.

❏ Reserve a meeting place and DVD equipment for the entire time. If the study will be done away from the church, select a location (home, for example) that is suited for the group you expect or hope to reach.

❏ Promote the study with women's ministry or other church leaders. A promotional segment is on the DVD, and bonus footage can also be used in publicity.

❏ Gather name tags, felt-tip markers, and pens or pencils. Enlist helpers as needed. Prepare a registration list for names, addresses, e-mails, phone numbers, and other information you would like.

❏ Assemble props to add interest to your meeting room: a large spotlight, a stool or chair, a pair of safety glasses or sunglasses, a set of headphones, a pair of men's shoes, a lightbulb, and a flexible light or large flashlight. Try to find a construction worker's hard hat to use the entire time. Look at "Before the Session" for suggestions unique to that session.

❏ Music can enhance a study. While hymns may be familiar to a churched group, consider contemporary Christian songs if targeting unchurched women.

❏ For your focal wall, download from LifeWay.com the house visual and the "Knowledge," "Understanding," "Wisdom," and "Good Sense" placards (see p. 164 for a diagram). Plan to display the house in every session.

❏ Enlist volunteers and prepare a schedule if you plan a refreshment time.

❏ Enlist additional facilitators if needed.

Your Role as Facilitator

As the facilitator, demonstrate your enthusiasm for the topic and excitement that the women have come together for this study. Lead with a positive attitude.

Choose questions that generate discussion among your group. One question in each session highlights a change in response based on the question "So What Do I Do?" or similar content. Encourage women to practice new ways of relating to their men.

Notice that activities highlighted ✔ are appropriate for singles. Decide whether you will group singles together or let groups form naturally. Be sensitive to singles while acknowledging that the primary application of this study is to marriage. You can help singles apply truths to the men in their lives at present (fathers, brothers, co-workers as well as boyfriends) and to their future husbands. Encourage married women to occasionally make other applications (to son or co-workers, for example).

Many topics covered in *For Women Only* are of a very personal nature. Encourage women in your group to share as they feel comfortable, but don't pressure anyone to reveal personal information.

During this study you may discover some wounded women. Be sensitive to anyone who might need to talk outside of the meeting. Know your limits, however. Ask for referral or help from church leaders for anyone who has needs too serious to deal with in the group.

Leading Group Discussion

1. Confidentiality is a vital part of this small-group experience and process. Ask the group to agree that what is shared in weekly sessions be held in strictest confidence.

2. Encourage women to share honestly about their struggles in relating to their men as their men need. Help them explore changes they can make by asking questions such as "What are some ways you can change your response to him, based on what you have learned?" "What could you have done differently (in a particular situation)?"

3. Encourage women to consider pairing up with an accountability partner. This partner could be a member of the group or someone else whom she trusts. Partners would pray daily for each other—praying together when possible—and hold each other accountable for the progress they are making toward their study goals.

4. As needed, remind women of the Ground Rules set in the Introductory session. Keep the discussion from turning negative. Avoid letting women make jokes about their husbands' abilities, for example.

Instead, purposefully direct women's attention to how to apply what they are learning to *their* thoughts, words, and actions. Then watch for ways for God will work in their lives.

5. If you encounter women who are hostile to some of the concepts, using "If" questions can help keep discussion flowing ("If this finding is true, what does that mean for us?")

Unraveling the Mystery of Manhood

Before the Session

1. Assemble name tags, markers, and pens or pencils.
2. Prepare a registration list with space for each participant's name, address, e-mail, and telephone number.
3. Assemble and display a few simple props: a large spotlight, a stool or chair, a pair of safety glasses or sunglasses, a set of headphones, a pair of men's shoes, a lightbulb, and a flexible light or large flashlight. Have the hard hat ready to use when needed.
4. Place the house visual on a focal wall and the placards nearby.
5. Invite someone to sing or play, "Open My Eyes That I May See" (*The Baptist Hymnal 1991*, No. 358) to close the session. Or, if yours is an unchurched group, use a contemporary Christian song about being open to God. Be sensitive to the level of church involvement; this can be a great outreach study.
6. If you plan a refreshment time, enlist volunteers and prepare a signup schedule.

During the Session

Welcome and opening remarks; video

1. Lead ladies to register, purchase workbooks, and fill out name tags as they arrive.
2. Welcome participants and open with prayer. Ask, *Does anyone have a boyfriend or husband, son, brother, father, or male coworker?* (All should have some.) As they introduce themselves, ask women to indicate whether they are single or married and, if married, for how long.
3. Highlight the schedule, process, and goals for this study. Holding up a lightbulb up, say: *I hope that each of you will have a lightbulb experience every week of our time together. The Lightbulb icon in your workbook alerts you to some truth about the inner lives of men.*

   As *lights come on for you, you can: (1) Discover how your man thinks and feels and what he needs from you; and (2) Examine your actions and attitudes for how to better meet his innermost needs. Great goals, aren't they?*

   Turn on the large spotlight and place items on the stool as you talk: *When you see the Spotlight icon, you will be trying to imagine what he sees in your actions (safety glasses) and hears in your words (headphones). Try to understand what it must be like to be in his shoes.*

   Holding up the flashlight, continue: *When you see the Searchlight icon in your workbook, the activity focuses on you. Just as you use a flashlight to find things, so will the Searchlight help you examine your thoughts, feelings, and motives in light of God's Word.*

4. Overview the format of the workbook (five days, activities), including features you just described and others like memory verses. Encourage women to set aside some time each day to think about their relationships with their men and with God.

   Direct them to the Week 1 introduction (pp. 8-9) and the Lightbulb truth that will guide them next week. Now ask them to turn to Day 1 of Week 1 (p. 10). Overview other days if needed.
5. Invite ladies to turn to the video viewer guide on page 7 and to meet Shaunti in the first video segment. Indicate they will learn about her research and the surprising revelations behind our study. After the video, make sure everyone filled in the appropriate answers.

   Ask women to share: *What was the most striking thing you heard in the video? Which part of this study sounds most challenging? What are you looking forward to most?*

   Emphasize the need for ground rules, especially confidentiality. Say, *Beginning next week we will share in small groups or in pairs so we can learn from each other. So it is especially important that what is shared in the group stays in the group.*

Debrief and conclude

6. Point to the house visual. Ask someone to read Proverbs 24:3-4 aloud from her Bible. Say, *You will be using all of this enlightenment or insight to build your "house"— your relationship with your man. You may need a hard hat some weeks when Shaunti's words seem hard to take! But in the end, the goal we all have is to fill our houses with the beautiful treasures that the Lord has in store for us.*
7. Thank women for attending and encourage them to return next week. Invite them to pray a prayer of commitment as they listen to the closing music. Encourage them to give God permission to open their eyes and change their minds as He sees necessary in the weeks that are ahead.

Proverbs 24:3-4

This house visual represents relationships we are building when knowledge, understanding, wisdom, and good sense are established logically. Use this motif as part of your focal wall each week. Make Knowledge, Understanding, Wisdom, and Good Sense placards to place over each level of the house starting with the foundation (Knowledge). When all are used together, be sure they are placed in proper sequence.

You may download this art at www.lifeway.com ("Bible Studies for Women"; search For Women Only).

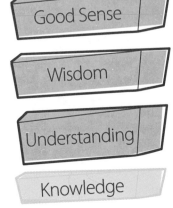

Good Sense

Wisdom

Understanding

Knowledge

Your Love Is Not Enough

Before the Session

1. Display the house visual and the spotlight and chair display used in the Introductory Session.
2. Prepare to write on a whiteboard or make a poster with the letters R-E-S-P-E-C-T written vertically.
3. Prepare discussion/activity assignments and be ready to clarify information. Look at options if you have more time available than an hour.

During the Session

Welcome and opening remarks; video

1. Greet the women as they arrive. Open with prayer. Welcome any newcomers. Make sure that each participant has a workbook and has registered. If you have new participants, briefly review the study material.
2. Ask whether women have questions related to their homework. Indicate that Shaunti, on video, can help.
3. Turn on the spotlight. Ask, *When you put your men in the spotlight this week, what did you learn was their foundational need?* Display the letters R-E-S-P-E-C-T.

   Ask, *Are you gaining a new understanding about the difference between respect and disrespect? Using these letters as a starter, share some phrases that indicate what you have learned about respecting our men this week.* For example: *Seek to meet his needs instead of satisfying my own.* Allow 3 to 4 minutes for brainstorming.
4. Ask women to turn to the viewer guide on page 33 and to fill in blanks during the Session 1 video. Ask the group to listen for their own Video Reflections that could add detail to the R-E-S-P-E-C-T chart. Be sure to ask for their ideas after viewing the video.

Discussion

5. Distribute assignments to cover the week's main points. If needed, move into smaller groupings as you have planned. Be prepared to fill in any gaps.

   ✔ a: Respect is sometimes seen as being earned by people who are worthy for what they have done. How does that differ from what you studied in Ephesians 5:33? Lead women to share one thing they appreciate about their men (p. 19).

   b: Talk about the respect Job received (Day 1). Which indicators are also important to your man? Describe how he must feel to be the object of high esteem.

   ✔ c: What are some roadblocks to showing our man the respect he needs?

   ✔ d: Read Job 30:9, NCV (p. 25). Were you surprised by how joking in public or teasing makes men feel? Why or why not? Lead women to share possible reasons women make these comments (p. 26).

   e: So What Do I Do?—Begin by trying to give "Better" responses in day-to-day situations (p. 30 activity). Changing the way we respond takes practice!

Debrief and conclude

6. Debrief assignments as a total group or by small-group reports. Provide more information as needed.

   If a group had assignment c, call on someone to share attitudes and actions they might need to change to better show respect for their man's abilities. Remind them that what is shared in the group is confidential and no one should feel pressured to share. As they do, however, they can encourage others.

   Share these "Better" responses for activity e: 1. No response, trust him; 2. "I would love for us to have time together. Could you help the children with their baths while I finish this project." 3. "Is there something you would like to do?" (Then do it gleefully!)
7. Repeat together the memory verse, Romans 12:1-2. Highlight verse 2 as the overall study verse.
8. Display the house outline. Say, *It is hard to build a house by yourself. This week you discovered that you are an important support to your husband.* Read Ecclesiastes 4:9-10 aloud. Say, *This verse also applies to us; we need to support each other in the weeks ahead.* Suggest that an accountability/prayer partner can be valuable.
9. As women join hands, lead in prayer for the group.
10. Dismiss by previewing Week 2. Say, *You already have begun work on your Weekly Challenge. If you need a reminder, look back to page 28 and go for it!*

If you have more time

Choose from these topics to expand your schedule:

✔ 1. What implications does Philippians 2:2-5 have for your actions as you try to show greater respect to your man?

2. Share the most important new fact (knowledge) or insight (wisdom) you have acquired this week.
3. How do the three stop signs about assumptions help you change your responses to your man? (p. 31)

✔ *appropriate for singles in the group*

The Performance of a Lifetime

Before the Session

1. Put the house outline on the focal wall. Use the spotlight and chair display from the Introductory Session.
2. Provide a paint can with a small amount of black tempera paint and a paintbrush. On white poster paper write the word *AFFIRM* with a white crayon.
3. Continue to use the hard hat and flashlight. Option: Use a R-E-S-P-E-C-T chart to review new knowledge.

During the Session

Welcome and opening remarks; video

1. Greet women as they arrive, and open with prayer. Ask newcomers to introduce themselves. Allow a few extra minutes for women to greet those they do not know.
2. Hold up the paint can and paintbrush. Say, *When you work on your house, paint comes in handy.* As you speak, paint over the poster paper so that the word *AFFIRM* is revealed.

   Say, *Paint can cover up scratches and imperfections on walls. A little paint can give a drab room a big boost in no time. Today we will talk about things you can do to boost your man's confidence.*
3. Ask women to turn to the viewer guide on page 57 and to view the Session 2 video. State this Video Reflection: Your support and affirmation can move your man from insecurity to self confidence.

Discussion

5. Distribute assignments to cover the week's main points. If needed, move into smaller groupings as you have planned. Be prepared to fill in any gaps.

✔a: Discuss insecurities you see in men based on the examples of Job and Moses. As you are comfortable, share a time you made a man feel more insecure, not less. (Day 2)

✔b: How does affirmation differ from flattery? Remembering that affirmation honestly reflects feeling, celebrates who the person is, and expresses appreciation—what are some steps you can take to affirm your man?

c: Share a time you used an opportunity to affirm your man and counteract his secret insecurity. How did he respond?

d: Read Hebrews 3:13 and I Thessalonians 5:11 and share the affirmation you chose to give your husband (p. 47). Did you begin sentences similar to "I appreciate that ...", "We are lucky that you...", "I trust you to ..."?

e: So What Do I Do?—Discuss ways a woman can create a safety zone where a man feels free from having to prove himself.

Debrief and conclude

6. Debrief assignments as a total group or by small-group reports. Clarify information as needed about insecurity and affirmation.
7. Put on your hard hat and hold the flashlight. Ask, *How are you doing? Is some of this new knowledge painful? Are you a little unsure about exercising the insights your are gaining?* Remind the group that when we are resistant to the purposes of God, we may need to look first at our own hearts. Ask but don't call for women to answer, *Is He asking you to make some changes?*

   Lead the women to repeat together the memory verse, Philippians 2:3-4.
8. Preview Week 3 by saying: *He may feel secretly insecure but he also feels a burden to conquer the world for us.* Read the Weekly Challenge and the Memory Verse (p. 59). Encourage women to work at memorizing Scripture. One idea is to place a card with the verse in their cars or purses or on a computer screensaver—wherever they might see it frequently during the day.
9. Ask women to pair up to read Colossians 3:12-13 and to pray. Encourage women to share something that might be standing in the way of showing respect and trust for their men, and then to pray for each other.

If you have more time

Choose from these topics to expand your schedule:

✔1. Shaunti uses the analogy of a boxer entering the boxing ring every day to talk about the struggle men face with their feelings. How can this analogy help you better understand and relate to your man (husband, coworker, father, son) and his insecurities?

2. Can you think of a time your feelings and rights got in the way of your man's feelings—either in what you said or in how you said it?

3. Practice being positive about men right now. Share something you admire about your man and something he always gets right.

✔ *appropriate for singles in the group*

The World on His Shoulders

Before the Session

1. Display the house outline, the spotlight, and the chair display used in other sessions.
2. Locate and display a large builder's level.
3. Have the Session 3 DVD ready to play.
4. Prepare assignment sheets. Make enough copies of the Lifestyle Evaluation (p. 171) for each woman.
5. Consider "If you have more time" options.

During the Session

Welcome and opening remarks; video

1. Greet women as they arrive and open with prayer.
2. Try to answer any questions about the homework.
3. Show the builder's level. Say, *When you are building a house, a level keeps everything on track. Walls are straight. Floors are level. Things go together as they should.* Turn on the spotlight and place the level on top of the other items in the chair. Continue: *Your man feels the pressure of keeping it all together. How well do you contribute to keeping your family lifestyle in balance?*
4. Ask women to turn to the viewer guide on page 83 and to watch the Session 3 video. Conclude with this Video Reflection: *Now women get it. Now we can be part of the solution instead of adding to his problem.*

Discussion

5. Distribute assignments to cover the week's main points. If needed, move into smaller groupings as you have planned. Be prepared to fill in any gaps.

✔a: How did your study of Scriptures this week help you understand a man's driving need to provide? Focus on Genesis 1 and 2; Exodus 35; and the Proverbs used in Days 1and 2.

b: Before this study, can you remember the last time you complimented your husband on one of his God-given talents? What was his reaction?

✔ c: How were you impacted by the discussion of love and time? Do you ever gripe about your man's work habits? How has your understanding changed?

d: Read Luke 12:22-26 and answer: What is God revealing to you about worry? How can your worry affect your man? What changes do you need to make?

✔e: So What Do I Do? New insights should bring about new actions and attitudes as you transform your thinking. Share some responses to the page 68 activity.

Debrief and conclude

6. Debrief assignments as a total group or by small-group reports. Clarify information as needed.
7. If the entire group has not discussed actvitiy e, ask whether anyone had problems coming up with action plans. Let the group make suggestions.

Affirm those who came up with such ideas as "I will remind myself that he feels pressure even when he doesn't show it." "I will not resent what I don't have." "I will show enthusiasm for something we have or do even though it's not my first choice." "I will show appreciation for the hard work he does."

8. Distribute the Lifestyle Evaluation and give women time to complete it. Help them enjoy scoring it with this scale: **21-30 = Storm clouds on the horizon** (You may be part of the problem.); **15-20 = Partly cloudy, rain likely** (Conflicts may often arise over finances.); **3-14 = Mostly sunny** (You're both on the same team.) Call for comments and reactions.

Discuss how the wisdom of Luke 12:13-31 can provide us the good sense and ultimately a better "forecast" in our relationship with our provider-husband.

9. Preview Week 4 by reading the Weekly Challenge and the memory verse on page 85.
10. Ask ladies to pair up to pray; they do not need to pray with the same partner they did last week. Ask each pair to read James 3:17-18. Each woman, as she feels free, can share one thing that stands in her way of putting his needs ahead of her own. After her partner prays for this need, the session is dismissed.

If you have more time

Use this idea to expand your schedule:

✔ Locate a copy of the music video, "American Dream" (*Live From Atlanta: Casting Crowns* CD/DVD.; 4:15 min.), for the "Debrief" portion of the schedule. Print words on a visual or overhead cel if you think women might have difficulty hearing the words.

Ask them to watch the video and jot down any reactions. The typical response is to blame this man for giving his all to his job and losing his family. Afterward, allow women to share their comments. and ask, *How would your reaction have been different before this study?*

✔ *appropriate for singles in the group*

Sex Changes Everything

Before the Session

1. Place the house visual on the focal wall and a construction hard hat nearby. Have the four placards ready to place on or near the house.
2. Write the following comments on separate index cards, and place them in a gift bag:
   - My husband wants to satisfy his physical urge and "get some" whenever he can.
   - My husband needs me to desire him and to be a responsive partner.
3. Have the Session 4 DVD ready to play.
4. Prepare assignments for discussion.
5. Consider "If you have more time" options.

During the Session

Welcome and opening remarks; video

1. Greet the women as they arrive. Begin with prayer.
2. Ask if anyone had questions about the homework.
3. Place the "Knowledge" placard on the bottom level of the house (or wall near the house) and the "Understanding" placard on top of it. Ask, *What new facts and insights about men did you acquire this week? What surprised you?*
4. Ask participants to turn to page 107 and to watch the Session 4 video segment. Summarize with this Video Reflection: Only you complete your husband. He deeply wants to be desired by you.

Discussion

5. Distribute assignments to cover the week's main points. If needed, move into smaller groupings as you have planned. Be prepared to fill in any gaps.

✔a: Respond to this statement: Something is missing in your husband, and only you can fill that void (p. 87). How does this truth differ from the popular view of a man's sexual needs?

b: Read Proverbs 12:4, *The Message* (p. 92). Discuss how a man feels when his advances for sex are rejected. How will this knowledge change your behavior?

✔c: First Corinthians 7:1-5 offers powerful warnings for couples. What principles does this passage teach? What temptations are ever-present for men?

d: Discuss "Gail's" example and ways it impacted you. Based on "Plan a Strategy for Change," how can you reevaluate your priorities?

✔e: What surprised you about a man's definition of romance? (p. 105) As you feel comfortable, share: What activities does your husband enjoy that might be romantic possibilities in *his* thinking?

Debrief and conclude

6. Debrief assignments as a total group or by small-group reports. Clarify information as needed.
7. Hold up the gift bag. Say, *You are a gift from God for your husband. Your husband is a gift from God to you. Sex is a gift God provides for both of you.*
   Ask two married women to open the gift bag, to remove one of the cards, and to read it aloud. Ask the group, *Which statement best summarizes the new understandings we need to gain this week?* Guide the group to respond that men need their wives to desire them.
8. Now pass the gift bag around the group. When the bag comes to her, anyone who wants to pray may voice a sentence prayer of thanksgiving or petition for the Lord's help. (Don't pressure anyone to pray.)
9. Put on the hard hat and comment: *You may want to put on your hard hat next week; you certainly will want God's guidance. You are about to gain some new wisdom and understandings about subjects we women take very personally. But don't overlook what may also be some new facts for you.* Read the Weekly Challenge (p. 109), commenting that it is designed to help us practice "good sense" as we honor God and our men.
10. Place the "Wisdom" and the "Good Sense" placards on the other two, with "Good Sense" on top. Encourage women to continue "establishing their homes." Dismiss and encourage women to return next week.

If you have more time

Choose from these topics to expand your schedule:

1. Read Proverbs 12:4, *The Message* (p. 92). What was your reaction to this verse? How do you better understand the impact of rejection on a man's inner core?
2. How did Shaunti's explanation of the lure of pornography change how you view that male temptation? In light of I Corinthians 7:1-5, what responsibility does a wife have to safeguard her husband?
3. Share any "beautiful treasures" you have added to your relationship as a result of this week's study.

✔ *appropriate for singles in the group*

Keeper of the Visual Rolodex

Before the Session

1. Set up the house visual, spotlight, and chair display. Continue to use the construction worker's hard hat.
2. From magazines and newspapers, clip pictures that represent day-to-day potential "triggers" for a man's mental Rolodex. During an hour's television program that men might watch, count the number of suggestive commercials.
3. Prepare assignments, considering expanded options.

During the Session

Welcome and opening remarks; video

1. Greet women as they arrive and open with prayer.
2. Ask if anyone has questions about the homework. Ask, *Who worked on your Weekly Challenge this week?* Shine the spotlight on these ladies and cheer!
3. Say, *I did some work myself on the Weekly Challenge.* Show the pictures you located and place them on top of the shoes in the display. Ask, *Were you surprised at the opportunities your man has to be bombarded by sexual images?* Encourage women to share about the "eye magnets" they discovered this week.
4. Ask the group to turn to the viewer guide on page 133 and to watch the Session 5 DVD segment. Sum up with this Video Reflection: A man's visual nature is very distracting and exhausting, even to the most godly, Christian man. He needs your support.

Discussion

5. Distribute assignments to cover the week's main points. If needed, move into smaller groupings as you have planned. Be prepared to fill in any gaps.
   a: You know that your husband appreciates beautiful women. In what ways do you see this as a burden with which he struggles rather than something he enjoys? How can you help him carry his burden? (see Gal. 6:2-5).
   ✔b: Talk about the progression of response that occurs when a man is visually stimulated. (Day 2) What are the differences between a man's response to visual temptation and a woman's? Are you reassured to know this is not about you? (Day 3)
   ✔c: Did you take the mirror test? Discuss what constitutes modest dress. Has this study changed your thinking on fashion and style?
   d: Discuss: "When you take care of yourself, I feel loved." (Day 4) If your husband had strong feelings about your appearance, do you think he would talk to you about it? Why or why not?
   e: Many men are able to honor their wives and God by exercising discipline over their visual temptations. Discuss the energy required for men to do this. Using the HALT checklist (p. 131), how do you see your responsibility as your husband's helpmate in relation to this list?

Debrief and conclude

6. Debrief assignments as a total group or by small-group reports. Put on your hard hat to clarify information in this important session. Briefly highlight the principles represented by each of the five assignments, especially if someone/some group did not report. Call attention to the prayer cards on page 132.
7. Preview Week 6 by asking, *How many of you are married to or have a "great" man in your life?* Say, *You know what some people say: "Behind every great man is a great woman." You are in for a blessing this week.* Read the Weekly Challenge and memory verse on page 135.
8. Consider adjusting the schedule next week to make it festive with refreshments or other special touches.
9. Guide women to pair up for prayer as they open their Bibles to Colossians 1:9-14. Say, *After I read this passage aloud as a prayer for you, use these verses to continue to pray for one another this week.*

If you have more time

Choose from these topics to expand your schedule:
1. How are you strengthened by the *agape* love in 1 Corinthians 13:4-7? How did this week's study help you work on your "house" with understanding, wisdom, and good sense?
✔2. The Bible says younger women are to learn from older, wiser women. What should we be teaching girls and teens about these issues?
✔3. How are your prayers being transformed as a result of this study? Discuss reasons the visual element is an important area in which to support your man in prayer. Ask for thoughts on the stories about Jim and Becky (pp. 122,131)

✔ *appropriate for singles in the group*

The Power of a Woman in Love

Before the Session

1. On a strip of paper write *www.lifeway.com*. Display the house visual (without placards) on the focal wall.
2. From magazines clip pictures of items that are part of a typical room, and place them in a basket at the front of the room. Option: Bring in actual accessories to create a home-like display in your meeting area: a side chair, a small table with a lamp, a vase of flowers, pillows, among other ideas.
3. Plan for refreshments in this session or in a later celebration event.
4. Option for expanded session: Gather construction or remodeling items: a yardstick, a level, a construction hat, a paint can, paintbrushes, a roll of wallpaper, a brick, spotlights, and flashlights.

During the Session

Welcome and opening remarks; video

1. Greet the women as they arrive, and enjoy refreshments together if part of your plans. Open with prayer.
2. Say, *You have been working hard at building up your relationship with your husband. Remodeling is well under way. Today we will hear about the treasures that are filling your spiritual rooms as a result of your study.*
3. Ask ladies to turn to the viewer guide (p. 158) and to watch the concluding celebrative DVD segment .

Discussion

4. Distribute assignments to cover the week's main points. If needed, move into smaller groupings as you have planned. Be prepared to fill in any gaps.
✔a: So, do you think men are unromantic clods or not? What is the basic stumbling block to a man's romantic initiative? How can you make sure your husband is built up when he puts himself out there to do something romantic? Look at verses from Romans 14 and 15 (p. 138). How did these verses strengthen you?
✔b: How can living by the principles in I Corinthians 10:23-24 give a woman the power to change her behavior? Can you think of instances in which you have had the good sense to apply these truths? What happened? Think about all the lightbulb experiences you have had about men, not just insights about romance.
✔c: So What Do I Do?—Turn to Day 4 Spotlight (pp. 151-53). What lightbulbs need to come in these

examples? What might these women do differently? Share answers using the list of seven revelations (p. 159) or the Lighbulb in each week's introduction.
✔d: On Day 5 you read about some women who are filling their spiritual rooms with treasures as they forsake selfishness and learn to honor their spouses. Talk about their stories, as well as any *you* could share.

Debrief and conclude

5. Debrief assignments as a total group or by small-group reports. Clarify information as needed.
6. Say: *I hope this has been a joyous week as you've heard encouraging words from men and life-changing stories from women. Who would share your story? As you share, choose a picture of a room furnishing or item.* After everyone who wants to has shared, lead women to arrange items so that the "house" is attractively decorated.
   Congratulate women on the good sense they are showing in applying their new knowledge, understandings, and wisdom. Say, *You are honoring God and making your relationships more meaningful and inviting.*
7. Thank ladies for participating in this Bible study. Post the Web address on the focal wall, and explain that ten Challenge Devotions may be downloaded at *www. lifeway.com* (click on Bible Studies for Women link) for anyone interested in building on what she has learned.
8. Conclude with prayer. Lead women to turn to the Day 5 Searchlight (p. 156) or to Matthew 6:9-13 in their Bibles. In pairs, guide them to pray this prayer, based on Jesus' Model Prayer, for each other.

If you have more time

1. Play the music video "The Man Inside of Me" (DVD 2, bonus). This song was written after the composer heard Shaunti speak about the inner lives of men. Allow women to share their thoughts after listening to the music.
✔2. Lead the group to sit in a circle. Pile the construction items on the floor in the middle of the circle. Ask each woman to choose an item and to tell what it brings to mind from the study. Reinforce the point that the principles they have studied are tools for better understanding the way God has created men. Encourage anyone who is willing, to share how a concept has changed her thoughts, words, and actions.

✔ *appropriate for singles in the group*

Improving Your Lifestyle Forecast

Answer the following questions Yes (*y*), Sometimes (*s*), or No (*n*). Tally the results to get a picture of possible provider issues. Tally your results using this point system: 3 points for each *Yes, often*; 2 points for each *Sometimes*; 1 point for each *No*.

___ 1. Do you ever hide your purchases from your husband/boyfriend?

___ 2. When you are depressed, do you shop to "feel better"?

___ 3. Does any of your sense of self-worth come from one or more of the following: how much money you make, where you live, what you wear, or what things you own?

___ 4. Do you find it hard to stick to agreed-upon limits?

___ 5. Do you find it difficult to trust God to meet your needs or your family's needs?

___ 6. Do you often make purchases that do not fit your budget?

___ 7. Do you buy items for your children so that they can "fit in" even when the purchase is not a good financial decision?

___ 8. Do concerns over money push you to unhappiness and resentment?

___ 9. Are finances at the heart of arguments between you and your husband/boyfriend?

___ 10. Do you make large purchases without consulting your husband or other family member?

MY TOTAL: _____

Interpreting Your Points

21-30 Storm clouds on the horizon

15-20 Partly cloudy, rain likely

3-14 Mostly sunny

You may be part of the problem. Conflicts may arise over financial matters. Your husband feels you're both are on the same team.

Proverbs 24:3-4

Before you speak or act, ask yourself:

- Will this draw us closer or drive us apart?

- Will it build up our relationship or tear it down?

- Will it cause destructive or constructive feelings?

- Does my thought or action express my love and loyalty to my partner, or does it reveal my own wants and desires?

"… be transformed by the renewing of your mind, …" (Rom. 12:2)

By nature, your heart turns from God and rebels against Him. The Bible calls this "sin." Romans 3:23 tells us, *"For all have sinned and fall short of the glory of God."*

Yet God loves you and wants to save you from sin, to offer you a new life of hope now and of eternal life in heaven. John 10:10 it tells us, *"I* [Jesus] *have come that they may have life and have it in abundance."*

You cannot achieve a personal relationship with God and this abundant life on your own. To give you this gift of salvation, God made a way possible through His Son, Jesus Christ. Romans 5:8 explains: *"But God proves His own love for us in that while we were still sinners Christ died for us!"*

You can receive this gift by faith in Jesus and faith alone, according to Ephesians 2:8-9: *"For by grace you are saved through faith, and this is not from yourselves; it is God's gift— not from works, so that no one can boast."*

Faith is a decision of your heart demonstrated by genuine repentance (turning away from sin) and changed actions in your life (turning to Jesus). Romans 10:9 says, *"If you confess with your mouth 'Jesus is Lord,' and believe in your heart that God raised Him from the dead, you will be saved."*

If you are choosing right now to believe Jesus died for your sins and to receive new life through Him, you can pray a prayer similar to the following, in which you accept what He has done for you and thank Him for your new life. This prayer is just an example.

> Dear God,
> I know that I am a sinner. I believe that Jesus died to forgive me of my sins. I accept right now Your offer of eternal life. Thank You for forgiving me of all my sin. Thank You for my new life. From this day forward, I will choose to follow You.

If this expresses the prayer of your heart, we want to help you grow as a new Christian. Tell your pastor or group leader about your decision.

Answers

Answers, Video Viewer Guides

Introductory Session

This study is about going from a *surface* understanding what it means in *practice*.

The Bible tells us … *knowledge, understanding, wisdom, good* sense.

What do wisdom and understanding do? *establish your home*

What do wisdom and knowledge bring? … *strength* and *power*

What does good sense do? … *priceless treasures*

Ground rules

3. We will talk about what is *common*
5. This study … intentionally *one-sided.*

Session 1: Your Love Is Not Enough

Recognize how *primary* and *important* respect is …
Our men most need … *respect, trust, admire*
We need to learn to love them in the *way* they need
"To sum up, each one of you is to *love* his wife as himself, and the wife is to *respect* her husband" (Eph. 5:33, HCSB).
Who must show *agapao* love … *Husbands*
Definitions: 2) "*reverence* , *venerate,* treat with *deference*"
Most of us don't know what it *looks like* …
The wife must *choose* to respect her husband …
When you … demonstrate respect, they feel *adored.*
She can *pierce his heart* …
… our thoughts and actions will begin to *change*.

Session 2: The Performance of a Lifetime

If indeed our man is not sure … *build him up.*
"I'm not sure" … paired with … always being *watched* and *judged* and *found wanting*.
He needs to know his wife … in his *corner*.
When you constantly ask … he may *hear* …
Do you say, *"Thank you …"*
Do you esteem him *highly*?
Do you … tell him, "I *know* you can do it!"
Are you patient with *him*?
He needs your *affirmation*.

Session 3: The World on His Shoulders
For a man, his drive to provide is a:
• *Burden* and *compulsion* …
Providing is *always* on his mind.
We can make the problem worse by being *critical*.

Guys run everything, … "Am I *providing adequately* …?"
• **Huge part of his *identity*;** "Our job … *IS* us!"
• **Way to do something *meaningful*;** they want to *change* the world.
• **Privilege**
• **Main way … "I *love* you";** no *choice*; appropriate response is *sympathy* …
• **Necessity;** … signals that "*stuff*" is more important; Talk to your husband … *lifestyle* you both want; *Appreciate* your man.

Session 4: Sex Changes Everything

For a man, sex fills a huge *emotional need* …
That … need is that his wife *desires* … and *wants* him.
If his wife responds out of *duty*, he feels *rejected*.
… "He is absolutely *desirable*; … "the *object* of desire"
Our husbands want *us* to want *them*.
The lure of pornography … the *message*
Give the physical relationship *priority*.
Making the first move … a *gift* …

Session 5: Keeper of the Visual Rolodex

Men are *visual* …
1. Even the most godly man faces this struggle.
    The issue is what he *chooses to do* …
    It is very *distracting*.
2. The image … is burned into his brain.
    They have to make the *distinction* between temptation and sin.
    … culture like for our men? *Exhausting*
    For Christian men, … *spiritual warfare*
    We can make his struggle worse by how we *dress; media; react*.
    It is emotionally important … *make the effort* …
    • They *hate this temptation* …
    • This struggle has *nothing to do* with us;
    • They really do want our *support*

Session 6: The Power of a Woman in Love

Men really do desire *romance* with their wives.
1. Guys often feel *clumsy* at romance … Whether or not they are romantic may be up to *us*.
2. We often miss their *signals* … why not learn to *enjoy*?
    They feel *handicapped* in telling us how very much they love us …
    Do you have a sense of the *power* God has given you?
    Change my mind, *open* my eyes, *show* me things …

Also from **Shaunti Feldhahn**

From the author who started it all, Shaunti Feldhahn brings to you life-changing resources to take the guesswork out of relating to the opposite sex. Surprising, eye-popping truths on every page!

For Women Only
What's going on in a man's mind? Take a look into the inner lives of men, and find guidance in providing the loving support that they want and need!

For Women Only 1-59052-317-2
Audio 1-59052-574-4

www.forwomenonlybook.com

For Men Only
Women: complicated and impossible to understand? Much to men's surprise, this book shows that women are actually not random and *can* be understood!

For Men Only 1-59052-572-8
Audio 1-59859-142-8

www.formenonlybook.com

What YOUNG WOMEN need to know about how guys think...

For Young Women Only Coming Soon!

Multnomah® Publishers
Keeping Your Trust...One Book at a Time®

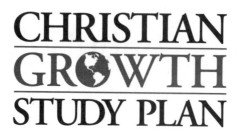

CHRISTIAN GROWTH STUDY PLAN

In the Christian Growth Study Plan (formerly Church Study Course), this book *For Women Only: The Bible Study* is a resource for course credit in the subject area Bible Studies of the Christian Growth category of plans. To receive credit, read the book, complete the learning activities, show your work to your pastor, a staff member or church leader, then complete the following information. This page may be duplicated. Send the completed page to:

Christian Growth Study Plan, One LifeWay Plaza Nashville, TN 37234-0117 • FAX: (615)251-5067 E-mail: *cgspnet@lifeway.com*
For information about the Christian Growth Plan, refer to the Christian Growth Study Plan Catalog. It is located online at *www.lifeway.com/cgsp*. If you do not have access to the Internet, contact the Christian Growth Study Plan office (1.800.968.5519) for the specific plan you need for your ministry.

For Women Only: The Bible Study
COURSE NUMBER: CG–1208

PARTICIPANT INFORMATION

Social Security Number (USA ONLY-optional) — — | Personal CGSP Number* — — | Date of Birth (MONTH, DAY, YEAR) — —

Name (First, Middle, Last) | Home Phone — —

Address (Street, Route, or P.O. Box) | City, State, or Province | Zip/Postal Code

Email Address for CGSP use

Please check appropriate box: ❏ Resource purchased by church ❏ Resource purchased by self ❏ Other

CHURCH INFORMATION

Church Name

Address (Street, Route, or P.O. Box) | City, State, or Province | Zip/Postal Code

CHANGE REQUEST ONLY

☐ Former Name

☐ Former Address | City, State, or Province | Zip/Postal Code

☐ Former Church | City, State, or Province | Zip/Postal Code

Signature of Pastor, Conference Leader, or Other Church Leader | Date

New participants are requested but not required to give SS# and date of birth. Existing participants, please give CGSP# when using SS# for the first time. Thereafter, only one ID# is required. **Mail to:** Christian Growth Study Plan, One LifeWay Plaza, Nashville, TN 37234-0117. Fax: (615)251-5067.

Revised 4-05